LIVING
with
PIGS

LIVING with PIGS

EVERYTHING YOU NEED TO KNOW TO RAISE YOUR OWN PORKERS

✳

Chuck Wooster

with photographs by **Geoff Hansen**

✳

The Lyons Press
Guilford, Connecticut
AN IMPRINT OF THE GLOBE PEQUOT PRESS

The Lyons Press is an imprint of the Globe Pequot Press.

Designed by LeAnna Weller Smith

Library of Congress Cataloging-in-Publication Data

Wooster, Chuck.
  Living with pigs : everything you need to know to raise your own porkers / Chuck Wooster and photography by Geoff Hansen.
    p. cm.
  Includes index.
  ISBN 978-1-59228-877-9
  1. Swine. I. Hansen, Geoff. II. Title.
  SF395.W66 2008
  636.4—dc22   2008003671

Printed in China
10 9 8 7 6 5 4 3 2 1

For Noel Perrin, whose writing about rural life continues to inspire me.

CONTENTS

ACKNOWLEDGMENTS

Thanks to Geoff Hansen, for getting us the gig and for doing justice to the many moods and expressions of the pig.

Thanks to Sue Kirincich, for living through the project with me, and to Sue, Kevin, Dan, Heather, Silas, and Louisa, for agreeing to live in close proximity with an ever-growing number of pigs.

Thanks to Carl Demrow, for his shining example of what it means to take responsibility for one's food.

Thanks to all the members and friends of Sunrise Farm, whose enthusiasm and support have revived one scrap of Vermont hillside and turned it into an honest-to-God, food-producing farm.

Finally, thanks to Olive the dog, for faithfully supervising every aspect of living with pigs and writing this book.

Why Pigs?

It's hard to know where to get started when talking about pigs. They're smart. They're funny. They're easy to raise. They're profitable. They're delicious.

They're also, in a sense, a contradiction.

No barnyard animal has a better nose, yet none smell worse. The pig has cloven hooves—an adaptation shared with flighty prey animals like sheep, deer, and antelope—yet no barnyard animal displays as much swagger or is less afraid. No animal is said to be smarter, yet pigs will stay out in the sun so long that they'll end up with second-degree sunburns.

The pig is the friendliest animal on the farm by far: always available for a scratch behind the ears, hardly ever moody, and quick with a grunt of delight. Yet the pig would also eat you for supper if the circumstances were right. Pigs are the only meat-eating animals that we, in turn, raise for meat.

The pig is synonymous with lard and fat and bacon, yet pork can be as fat-free as chicken or lean beef.

The pig is said to be the cleanest animal on the farm, yet every child knows that a pig will roll in a mud puddle at the first opportunity. Pigskin is one of the toughest and most useful of animal hides, yet it's sensitive to temperature and injury. Some breeds of pigs grow ferocious-looking tusks yet prefer to dine on roots and vegetables.

As if that's not enough, agriculture itself could scarcely have evolved eons ago without

Opposite: A curious pig pokes its snout between boards of a portable pen at Luna Bleu Farm in South Royalton, VT. The pig is the friendliest animal on the farm by far.

Above: Suzanne Long greets her hogs while feeding them at Luna Bleu Farm. The farm sells organic pork as part of its community-based operation.

the versatile pig, yet fewer and fewer farmers raise even a single pig these days. In 1965 more than a million farms in the United States had pigs. Today that number is down to 75,000.

At the heart of these discrepancies is a relatively straightforward fact: The pig is an omnivore. No other livestock animal has such a wide-ranging and catholic appetite. Pigs will eat anything and everything on the farm, from grain

and vegetable scraps to roots, shrubs, meat—even your lawn.

The pig is the original recycler, which is why pigs were the first animals to be domesticated back at the dawn of agriculture. Food that is no longer fit for consumption by people or other animals (spoiled hay, rancid milk, garden scraps) are all delights for the accommodating pig, who happily takes everyone else's castoffs and turns them into bacon, sausage, and ham.

Besides recycling, the pig is prized for its earth-moving abilities. Does a new pasture need stumping? Give it over to a drift of pigs, and their rooting and digging in search of tasty morsels will have shredded the small stumps by summer's end and made the larger ones easier to dig out. Too many weeds and weed seeds in the vegetable patch? A season's worth of pig digestion will help solve the problem. Have a daunting pile of winter manure in the barn that needs to be addressed? Drill some grain down into the bedding, turn the pigs in, and you'll have light, well-turned compost in a month or so.

But with most farm energy and fertilizer now being derived from fossil fuels, the pig's central role as recycler and earthmover has been eclipsed. This is a shame, because pigs are much easier to raise now than they once were, thanks to the invention of the electric fence.

These days, the lowly pig is making a major comeback. Part of it is the growing realization that fossil fuels have many hidden costs. Part of it is a renewed enthusiasm for local, fresh foods. But the biggest reason is simply the taste of fresh, pasture-raised pork. It's unbelievably good. The flavor explodes on your tongue. Even the most skeptical visitors to our house ("Isn't all pork the same?") come away amazed.

Before I'd tasted fresh, pasture pork, and before we'd purchased our first sounder of shoats (the technical term for a group of recently weaned piglets), I was reluctant to try raising pigs. I had the idea that pigs were unwieldy, smelly, and too smart by half. That their meat wasn't really that good for you. That trichinosis was lurking around the corner. That other animals were easier to raise.

I was wrong on all counts. Very wrong. With the zeal of the newly converted, I now see a place for pigs in most every backyard. As the local agriculture movement gathers momentum, the pig deserves to be at the very center of it.

Here's the moment when I was truly smitten by living with pigs. It was near the end of our first summer raising them. My sister's wedding reception was to be held on our farm, and I was tidying things up and making a final pass with the lawn mower when, out of the corner of my eye, I saw unexpected movement. I looked up to see our three 250-pound hogs casually sauntering across the lawn, headed straight for the party tent. They had somehow managed to unhinge the metal gate on their pen, cross an intervening pasture, and come over to get a leg up on the festivities.

Although my immediate concern was keeping the pigs separated from the hors d'oeuvres, I couldn't help but notice how those pigs carried themselves: confidently, with enthusiasm, heads held high, and ready for a night on the town. They all but had their party hats on. Here was an animal that knew how to enjoy life. I've been a big fan of pigs ever since.

ABOUT THIS BOOK

This book does not pretend to be the comprehensive guide to everything pig. For one thing, only cursory attention is paid to medical care or veterinary requirements. For another, no mention is made of pig breeding, farrowing, or any of the myriad details related to keeping pigs year-round and

Above: Yorkshire cross hog Maxene, left, takes a sniff at LaVerne after a roll in the mud at Sunrise Farm in Hartford, VT. The pig is said to be the cleanest on the farm but jumps into the muck at the first opportunity.

birthing piglets. These are not oversights; rather, they are subordinate to the main objective of this book: encouraging you to discover the joys, and delights, and simplicity, of living with pigs.

Most people who keep pigs do not keep them year-round, for the simple reason that young feeder pigs are relatively easy to buy. Unlike sheep or cows, which typically give birth to one or two offspring at a time, sows can give birth to a dozen or more piglets, twice per

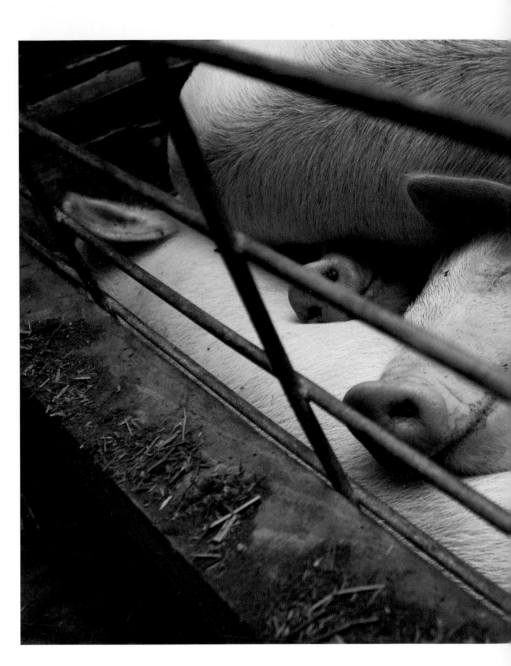

 Above: Weaned piglets nap in a pile at North Hollow Farm in Rochester, VT. Hardly ever moody, pigs are quick with a grunt of delight.

Above: Zola, a two-month-old registered female Tamworth, roams the pasture at Hogwash Farm in Norwich, VT. Given time, pigs can be as effective on a pasture as any motorized tiller.

year. Where a shepherd with a few ewes will only have enough lambs for home consumption, a farmer with a few sows can keep a dozen friends and neighbors supplied with shoats. Why raise them when you can easily buy them?

This is doubly true because the bulk of porcine veterinary care is tied up in breeding and farrowing. A healthy shoat, meanwhile, the kind I will encourage you to buy, will likely require no medical care of any kind in the five to six months that it will be in your care. None. Plus there's no winter feeding to worry about, and no need to maneuver 600-pound boars and sows around during the winter.

This isn't to say that keeping sows and boars for breeding isn't a wonderful endeavor and one that may well be waiting for you in the future. But it obscures the fact that living with pigs for the summer can be amazingly simple. Be a farmer if you want to and go whole hog—keep your own boars and sows—but only if you have the acreage and temperament. Whatever you do, however, don't miss the joy of having a few pigs in your life each summer. Living with pigs is simple, profitable, hilarious, and profound. And easy. This book will show you how to go about it.

Below: Vicky Parra Tebbetts's lone pig creamer is mixed in with her husband's collection of the bovine variety at their home in Cabot, VT.

HARRIS ON THE PIG: PRACTICAL HINTS FOR THE PIG FARMER

I have chosen to open every chapter of this book with a short, topical quote from Joseph Harris, the same Harris of the famous Harris Seed Company and the author of *Harris on the Pig* in 1870. (Was he proud or mortified by the title? He insisted that the publisher had thrust it upon him.) I love how these quotations anchor pigs in the long river of agriculture, emphasizing that pigs have been right with us all along. I also love how these quotes demonstrate that the essentials of raising pigs—good food, dry shelter, plenty of water, lots of dirt—have not changed over the centuries.

For those who want to enjoy Harris's writing for themselves, Lyons Press brought out an edition in 1999, with a foreword by Noel Perrin (ISBN 978-1558219786).

LIVING
with
PIGS

CHAPTER ONE

Buying Piglets

Of all the desirable qualities in a pig, therefore, a vigorous appetite is of the first importance.

—JOSEPH HARRIS

Few scenes in life are as hilarious and engaging as watching piglets. One minute they're asleep in a pile, occasionally squirming and wriggling closer to the center of the heap. The next they're up, scampering about, testing and probing everything that comes their way, snorting and rooting with their rubbery noses, taking the occasional nip or bite out of anything and everything that seems promising.

But the funniest moments of all, the times when my nose and ears practically burst as I try to contain my laughter (so as not to scare them off), is when piglets all come to a sudden, immediate stop and stand perfectly still, as if by prearranged signal. It's almost like the children's game of "red light, green light," when the person who is "it" wheels around suddenly to try to catch one of their friends still moving.

I can't tell if they're trying to catch me in the act, catch one another, or catch someone or something else that has come onto the scene, but the image of a bunch of piglets, milling and scampering about, suddenly freezing in place

Opposite: Newborn piglets—who are a mixture of Gloucestershire Old Spots, Landrace, and Tamworth—play in the barnyard at The Reimanis Farm, owned by Erik and Kate Reimanis, in South Strafford, VT. A playful piglet is a happy piglet, perfect for raising.

as a group, stock-still, all eyes on you, is unbelievable funny. It's like walking into a basement, flicking on the light, and finding a bunch of teenagers all staring at you, having just whipped the beer bottles behind their backs and managing to look both innocent and guilty at the same time.

This freeze-frame can last for three or four seconds, until one of the piglets will let out a grunt, another one or two will concur, and the group will slowly return to action, warily at first but then with growing confidence and swagger. Their activities will build in excitement for several minutes until one or two will somehow lose themselves, cross an invisible threshold, go over the top. The prearranged signal will go out, the group will instantly freeze in place, all eyes on you, and you'll have to do everything in your power not to let out such a howl of laughter that they all go scampering into a far corner to hide.

These are happy piglets. These are the kind of piglets you want to buy.

THINGS TO LOOK FOR IN A PIGLET

First and foremost, you want to buy piglets that seem energetic. You may think, "How am I going to recognize that a piglet is energetic and happy?" Have confidence that you will. Healthy piglets are happy piglets, and happy piglets are active and alert (when they're not actually asleep). If a piglet looks droopy and tired, is asleep while its littermates are up and about, has a dull, listless look to it, or has eyes that lack curiosity and sparkle, that piglet is not likely to be healthy.

This is not necessarily the case with other animals. Lambs, for example, are big sleepers, and it's perfectly normal for some lambs to be sleeping while others are playing. Dogs, too, display a wide range of personalities; my wife and I deliberately chose a sleepy puppy because we thought it would grow into a dog that would be relaxed and calm in adulthood. But these considerations shouldn't be applied to piglets; ultimately, you're looking for enthusiastic animals that are going to thrive and grow quickly.

Along the same lines, you also want to avoid buying a piglet that is substantially smaller than its littermates. This may be the runt of the litter (often the last one to be born), or may just be one that is not thriving and

Above: Gloucestershire Old Spots piglets contentedly nap in the barn at North Hollow Farm. Piglets can go from napping to running in a moment's notice.

taking life by the horns. Either way, this size discrepancy is unlikely to sort itself out as time goes on: A small piglet turns into a small hog.

There are a few specific medical maladies that you also want to look for and avoid. First is runny eyes, like conjunctivitis. This isn't necessarily a problem in itself but is an indication of a piglet with a less than robust immune system; same with any sniffles or wheezing or signs of respiratory ailment. Next is any obvious deformations or irregularities, especially cracks or malformations in the hooves. These are going to get worse, not better, with time.

The fourth medical malady to look for is any kind of bump or lump along the abdominal midline where the umbilical cord was attached. If the cord wasn't cleaned or handled properly during the first few days of life, the piglet can be beset by either infection (if the cord wasn't snipped and cleaned) or a hernia (if the cord was pulled or chewed, often by the sow, with enough force to damage the abdominal wall). Picking out an abnormal lump can be difficult on a male piglet because of the penis, but the penis's sheath should be symmetrically formed and about the size of a marble (with a little tuft of hair protruding). If there's a bump nearby or the flesh around the penis appears malformed, stay away. Otherwise, you might as well look up the vet's phone number right away.

This brings up the question of castration of male piglets, and the answer is "yes," make sure the males have been castrated. Excessive testosterone can give pork a gamey (and typically undesirable) flavor. The lads will grow nearly as fast without their nuts, and they won't waste energy later in the fall harassing any females in the vicinity. The piglet farmer usually performs this minor surgery at about four weeks of age, before you appear on the scene (usually at six to eight weeks).

Pig Nomenclature

A *piglet* is a baby pig that is still nursing.

A *shoat* is a recently weaned piglet.

A *barron* is a castrated shoat.

A *gilt* is a female shoat.

A *feeder pig* is a catch-all category for pigs that are bigger than shoats but smaller than hogs.

Hogs are anything 120 pounds and up, not counting breeding stock, which would be *sows* and *boars*.

Opposite: Nancy LaRowe scratches a Tamworth piglet at Hogwash Farm. After working in restaurants as a manager and server, LaRowe has been raising pigs for seven years. "I love them," she said. "They're great."

Above: Frannie, a "Heinz 57" mixed-breed sow, naps while her two-month-old piglets roam the barnyard at Luna Bleu Farm. Hybrid hogs usually lead to more rapid growth than the purebred variety.

A group of pigs is usually referred to as a *herd* these days, but the more descriptive, older terms are *drift* (which reminds me of how pigs move across the land—low down and packed together) and *sounder* (which is how pigs keep track of one another in thick brush—by snorting back and forth).

Back to buying piglets. In summary, these are the key attributes you should look for: happy, alert, large (or, not small) animals that are free of the obvious deformities. Piglets with these attributes are apt to live healthy lives and have excellent immune systems. You'll never have a need to call the vet.

One additional consideration: I keep referring to "piglets" here because I strongly recommend that you buy and raise more than one at a time. Two piglets is a minimum, three (or more) even better. Pigs are social animals, preferring company and crowds to the quiet, contemplative life. They'll be happiest with companions to wrestle with during the day and sleep in a pile with at night. Then, of course, there's a practical consideration: Pigs that are motivated by friendly competition will eat with more enthusiasm and gain weight more rapidly than a solo pig that's free to be picky.

There's always more to look for in a piglet, of course, and an experienced purchaser might take into account the condition of the sow and boar, the breed of pig, conformation issues such as the relationship of haunch to belly (meat breeds tend to be hourglass-shaped when viewed from the top—wider at the hams and shoulders—while the lard breeds look more barrel-shaped), and a host of minor characteristics that are invisible to the untrained eye. That's fine. If you have someone with an experienced eye who can accompany you on pig pickup day, so much the better.

Some people prefer to buy barrons, some gilts. I can't say that I've noticed a difference, or, put another way, I've found that a vigorous shoat of one sex will always do better than a less-than-vigorous shoat of the other sex. One thing to note: Both barrons and gilts have teats on their bellies, so you can't use that to tell them apart. The best way to do that is to notice the tuft of hair that protrudes from the penis sheath of the barron. Also, any barron you're wanting to buy should have the obvious twin scars on its hindquarters from castration.

But otherwise, don't sweat these details—they are less important than the basics I mentioned above, and you certainly don't want to buy a droopy and sick-looking piglet just because it happens to be of a certain breed. Most of the piglets you find for sale are of the Heinz 57 variety anyway, which is just fine. You're not looking to get into the pig-breeding business (at least at this juncture). You're just looking for some happy oinkers to raise out back for the summer, and all breeds are going to produce a pile of both ham and bacon.

FROM WHOM TO BUY?

As with most every other type of livestock, the best answer to this question is "your trusted neighbor." Especially if you're new to living with pigs, it's very handy to have someone nearby who knows the ropes—not because the ropes are particularly difficult, but because there's nothing like a reassuring "You're doing great!" every now and again. If this neighbor is the person who sold you the piglets in the first place, then they'll be eager to see you succeed and motivated to lend a hand. I would recommend choosing a trusted neighbor over any other consideration of breed or price (okay, within reason), especially in your first few years of raising piglets.

The next consideration is to find a farmer who believes in raising natural, free-range, medication-free animals. It's surprisingly common to find farmers who wean their piglets onto medicated feed, especially farmers who raise piglets in large quantities. The thinking is that the antibiotics are an insurance policy for the young piglets, helping to keep them healthy during their early, vulnerable weeks when they're all packed in together. But whatever benefit this may provide for the farmer is only going to create a burden for you, since you'll be getting a piglet whose immune system has been compromised by antibiotics and who is unaccustomed to the type of non-medicated feed you'll be serving.

The first few years I had piglets, I bought them from a largish operation that churned out dozens of piglets per month in the spring. All were weaned on medicated feed, and none had ever seen the light of day before coming home with me. These piglets had to deal with the triple shock of going to a new place, dropping their antibiotics, and learning about the great outdoors all at once. The fact is, they all made the transition pretty well and went on to thrive (except for one, whom we called "Wheezer" for the raspy breathing that he never managed to shake). But the transition seemed much more traumatic for them than for the piglets I've purchased more recently, who only have to deal with moving to a new place.

Some folks, of course, will respond to my advice by saying, "Just keep raising them on medicated feed—they'll grow faster anyway." But why would you want to do that? If medicated meat is what you're after, you can easily buy it at the supermarket. One of the joys of raising pigs is knowing where your meat came from, knowing that it is as natural and safe as can be. Pigs have grown and thrived for millennia without eating medicated feed, and they'll happily do the same at your place.

Above: With a treat of stale bagels nearby, a Tamworth piglet happily nurses from its mother at Hogwash Farm. Happy and alert piglets are a good sign of a hog that will live without problems needing a veterinarian's attention.

Above: Pam the Yorkshire sow rests while her litter nurses at North Hollow Farm. Yorkshire is one of the most common breeds of pigs in the United States.

What brand of feed have the shoats
  been eating? Is it medicated?
Have the males been castrated?
When were the shoats last de-wormed?
Have the tails been docked?
What breed (or mix of breeds) are the
  shoats?

BREEDS

Of all livestock, pigs are the most likely to be a mixture of many different breeds. While purebred sheep and cows and goats are more common than not, purebred pigs are the exception, not the rule. Nevertheless, you may find yourself in the enviable position of having multiple sources of healthy, happy piglets in your neighborhood. If so, a few words about pig breeds are in order. Though there are more than five dozen generally recognized breeds out there (and many more that are not officially recognized), these are the most common breeds in North America:

*   **Yorkshire**—This is what most people think of when they picture a pig: pinkish skin, large in size, white bristles, upright ears, no spots. Wilbur of *Charlotte's Web* fame was a Yorkshire—at least by the time Hollywood got a hold of him. Yorkshires are thought to have the best mothering instincts of all pigs, making Yorkshire crosses among the most commonly available piglets.

- **Chester White**—A slightly smaller cousin of the Yorkshire; the distinguishing feature are ears that flop forward instead of standing straight up. This is an American breed, developed in Pennsylvania in the early nineteenth century.

- **Landrace**—Another Yorkshire, all-white look-alike. In this case, the big, distinctive, droopy ears flap forward in front of the eyes, which, in combination with the breed's long torso, make it seem like a long, white tube on legs.

Above: Cookie, a Duroc cross sow, sniffs at new sawdust bedding with her piglet. Cookie was bred with a Landrace boar at Fat Rooster Farm.

- **Lacombe**—A shorter, stockier version of the Landrace that was developed in Alberta and remains popular, especially in Canada.

- **Berkshire**—A black pig with upright ears whose extremities (nose, tail, feet) appear to have been dipped in white paint. Besides the Yorkshire, no breed is more important than the Berkshire, whose large size and excellent meaty qualities are the foundation for many hybrid crosses.

- **Poland China**—A black pig with white extremities like the Berkshire, yet with droopy ears that fall toward the eyes. The shape of the Poland China is to the Berkshire what the Landrace is to the Yorkshire.

- **Hampshire**—A black pig with a white band around the front flank and forelegs—very distinctive and easy to recognize. Along with the other "-shire" pigs, the Hampshire is of English descent.

- **Duroc**—The most common all-red pig— really red, not pink—the Duroc is another breed that was developed in America in the nineteenth century.

Besides these common breeds, there are an increasing number of heirloom breeds available. As agriculture became more industrial in the middle part of the twentieth century and hog raisers focused increasingly on Yorkshire and Berkshire bloodlines, many of the more unusual pig breeds to have emerged began to fall by the wayside. In the past few decades, however, whether for fun or for issues of food security (not wanting to put all your proverbial eggs in one basket), these heirloom breeds have begun to recover their popularity, not with the big, industrial operations but with backyarders like you and me. If your trusted neighbor is raising one of these breeds, so much the better. (If not, you might want to seek out one of these breeds after a year or two of gaining experience closer to home. For starters, try the website of the American Livestock Breeds Conservancy, at www.albc usa.org.)

- **Tamworth**—All red, with a long, meaty frame and a relatively long, pointed snout. Tamworths are thought to be good mothers and thrifty eaters, though perhaps not as outstandingly meaty as many of the Berkshire crosses.

- **Gloucestershire Old Spots**—Lots of pigs have spots, especially those descended from the Berkshire bloodline, so spots usually indicate a crossbreed. Nevertheless, the English Gloucestershire Old Spots is a recognized, mostly white breed with several black spots, usually on the back and flanks.

Above: A pile of heritage breed Tamworth piglets bask in the winter morning sun at Hogwash Farm. While Tamworths don't grow as quickly as pigs raised on factory farms, their meat has more flavor due to a higher fat content.

- **Large Black**—As the name implies, an all-black and large, meaty breed that originated from Chinese and European breeding stock brought together in England. Some have been imported in recent years to North America.

As I mentioned before, you're most apt to find shoats that are a cross between two or more breeds. From a meat-growing perspective, this is good. Hybrid vigor (the combination of genetics from more than one

Above: Chili, a Tamworth and Large Black sow, gave birth to her piglets outdoors before LaRowe had a chance to move her closer to the barn at Hogwash Farm. After surrounding the area with an electric fence, the mother and twelve babies did well outdoors for three weeks. But LaRowe said it was a "logistical nightmare" to move them later for de-worming.

breed) usually leads to more rapid growth and larger ultimate size than the offspring of either purebred line. Purebred animals are important for folks who are raising piglets from birth and need to maintain bloodlines but are not important to you as the backyard hog raiser. Around our part of Vermont, if you ask someone what breed their piglets are, they usually say something like, "Well, mostly Yorkshire, of course, but there's certainly some Spot in there, and some of them do come out reddish in each litter, probably Tamworth." Excellent.

TAIL DOCKING

Should your shoats have had their tails docked? I don't think it matters much, though ideally, no. Commercial hog raisers are in the habit of docking piglet tails in order to keep the tails from caking up in manure. Also, pigs have the habit of biting one another's ears and tail when they are stressed, so removing the tail removes the temptation. On the other hand, a curly pig tail is a delightful appendage, and one that the pig will use to display emotion; a curly tail is said to be the sign of a contented pig. I've never had any trouble, with my happy, out-of-doors pigs, of either tail biting or tail caking. But I've certainly had a lot of fun watching those tails curl up as I approach the pen with a bucket of food. So buy shoats with long tails if you can find them.

CHAPTER TWO

The First Few Weeks

It is, nevertheless, a fact, that there is no more docile or tractable animal
on a farm than a well-bred pig.

—JOSEPH HARRIS

Shoat pickup day is always memorable. The only thing cuter than a couple of shoats in a pile is a whole bunch of shoats in a pile, and with luck, your pig farmer will have bunches of shoats to see and choose among.

There's also the surprising size difference between a sow and a piglet, which is far greater than with any other livestock animal. A mature sow may weigh 400 pounds or more, while her newborn piglets will weigh in the 2- to 4-pound range. That means the sow can be 200 times larger than a piglet—an extraordinary difference that helps explain why accidental crushing is a serious risk for young piglets. Watching the sow maneuver among the piglets is like watching the *Queen Mary* trying to dock amidst a flotilla of canoes; you can't help but cover your eyes whenever a little guy mistakenly cuts across her bow.

The shoats you'll be picking up, however, will be larger than that—usually between six and eight weeks old, fully weaned, and weighing 20 to 30 pounds each. That will make them a little less than 2 feet long. Your goal is to get them home safely and comfortably. Their

Opposite: LaVerne and Maxene, three-month-old Yorkshire cross shoats, enjoy spring turnips and lettuce atop their daily grain ration at Sunrise Farm.

goal is to stick together as tightly as possible, never losing contact with their kin during the uncertainties of the move.

TRANSPORTING THE SHOATS

Options for transporting your shoats home range from turning them loose in the back of a pickup truck to holding them on your lap in the car to putting them in a secure box or sack. Of all these options, using a secure box or sack is by far the preferred approach.

A cardboard box, 2 feet by 2 feet by 2 feet, will easily hold three shoats. Put a piece of plastic on the bottom in case they pee during the trip, and pack in 3 inches of straw or hay for bedding. Pop the shoats in, close and tie down the lid, and away you go. Although they will smell "piggy," unless it's a warm day, I think the journey is easier on the shoats if the box is inside the car instead of out in the noise and wind of a pickup truck bed. You can crack a window for air as needed.

Of course, a bigger box is fine. We've been using an old TV box for a few years now, having reinforced the corners and bottom with duct tape. But the shoats don't need the extra space. They're going to be sufficiently stressed by being moved that they're going to huddle together in a group. If you gave them a box big enough to hold a refrigerator, they'd still just huddle in the corner. So use whatever box is easy to fit inside the car.

Another good option is a dog crate or cage, solid sides being even better than metal lattice. (The shoats want to pretend it's not happening, so a dark, safe place is better than a wide-open view.) A third option is a burlap sack, provided you have space for at least two shoats per sack to keep one another company. Pop in the shoats, tie off the sack with a piece of rope or twine, and off you go. This is much less barbaric from the shoats' perspective than from yours: They're after close contact and minimal stimulation, and a dark sack fits the bill very well.

Regardless of which container you use, it's better to keep the shoats confined than to let them run free in the car or truck. Shoats are difficult to catch, and chasing them around adds needless stress to an already stressful

Above: Fresh from rooting in the barnyard dirt, an eight-week-old shoat wanders in its pen at Luna Bleu Farm. Food is important in helping a shoat feel comfortable in its new home.

day. You're going to need to unload them once you arrive home, so keep them contained in the meantime.

Materials to Have Before Pickup Day

box, sack, or cage for transportation

8x8-foot pen, with partition for crowding

bucket or pail for water

feeding trough with low sides

food (ideally same brand as the breeder
   used) mixed with milk

clean straw for bedding

THEIR FIRST PEN

Regardless of where your shoats are going to ultimately live, I strongly recommend that you keep them in a small, sturdy pen for the first week or two of their tenure. The reason is this: If the shoats escape now, you'll never see them again. Even ungreased pigs are impossible to catch in the open field. Throw in the fact that they don't yet know and trust either you or their new home, and they'll probably head for the hills out of fear. Your only recourse will be to wave good-bye as they disappear.

For housing two or three shoats, an 8x8-foot pen is fine. Tack together some old pallets or pieces of plywood at least 3 feet tall. (Shoats can travel in the vertical dimension in ways that hogs cannot, so your pen needs to be taller now than it will need to be later.) Or better yet, create an enclosure in the inside corner of your garage, shed, or outbuilding; anyplace sheltered and secure is perfect. Throw down a few inches of straw or hay for bedding and warmth, and you'll have a shoat palace.

Your goal during this transitional period is for the shoats to learn to recognize and trust you and associate you with good things happening. Once this is the case, they won't run away from you if they escape. They may even come over to see you and allow you to lead them back into their pen or pasture. But at the very least, they won't vanish in the woods, never to be seen again. Instead, they'll look to see what food and excitement you have to offer.

Food is the key to establishing this trust. Whenever I feed the shoats, I make grunting and snuffling noises similar to the ones they make while eating. I really go for it—carrying on like a happy pig. They quickly come to associate my grunting with fresh food, and within a week, simply grunting with enthusiasm will cause my shoats to jump up and come over to see what I'm offering. This is stage one of the acclimatization.

Opposite: A Yorkshire cross shoat drinks milk at Fat Rooster Farm. During the first week, feed a shoat primarily grain soaked in milk to help its digestive tract adjust to the new surroundings.

Stage two is to get them comfortable with being handled. This is somewhat harder, since most shoats will happily come near you if food is at hand but will craftily move just out of arm's reach if you show any intention of touching them. To solve this, I've made a portable partition

Above: Zola, an eight-week-old Tamworth shoat, noses into a stream filling a water bucket at Hogwash Farm. A clean pen makes it easier to handle shoats as they get used to your company.

that I use to confine the shoats into a corner where I can easily scratch their backs and rub behind their ears without them getting away. The partition is nothing more than two 4-foot-wide wooden gates connected with hinges. I fold it up and lash it to the side of the pen between feedings.

At feeding time, I step into the pen, crowd the shoats behind the partition, tie the partition to the pen wall to keep it in place, and step in to scratch their backs and ears. After a few minutes of this, once they relax and calm down, I go into the grunting and snorting routine in preparation for feeding them. Then I'll give them some food right there inside the partition—either some vegetables or bread or something easy, or even their full feeding if there's space. Only then will I remove the partition and give them full access to the pen. Typically, they never even notice, being fully engaged in eating.

Tight confinement is the key: If you have to chase the shoats to catch them, you're only training them to flee whenever they see you. Your goal is the opposite—training them to run *to* you whenever they see you.

After four or five days of this procedure—crowding, handling, feeding—the effect is profound: The pigs associate me with food and being petted, both of which they come to think of as being good things. Once this behavior is established, I transition to handling and feeding them without crowding them behind the partition. After another four or five days, they should be fully acclimated to me and show no fear (assuming I make no sudden movements). This lays a great foundation for working with the animals as they grow up and become 300-pound, otherwise unmanageable hogs.

WHAT TO FEED THE SHOATS

For the first few days after their arrival, your shoats may not eat very much, especially if they've just been de-wormed before arriving at your place. Make sure they have continual access to fresh water to keep from becoming dehydrated. I find that an anti-tip-over dog's water bowl is best for this; if it's placed on flat ground, the shoats will be unable to tip it over. They'll wade in often enough, so just dump out the dirty stuff from time to time and replace with fresh water.

The best feed to give them for this first week is whatever they were eating at their original home. Whether it's mash, crumble, or pellets, add in water or, better yet, milk to soften it up. (A gallon of store-bought milk is well worth it at this point, assuming you don't otherwise have access to spoiled milk or other dairy products.) Almost any old feeder will work, provided the sides are no more than a few inches high so that the shoats can easily reach in. I use an old oven roasting pan for the job, which has 1-inch-tall sides and easily holds enough food for a four-shoat feeding. The shoats walk in and trample things, so just scrape out the leavings between feedings.

This is also a good time to start them on leftover bread, pancakes, vegetables, or whatever yummy treats are coming down the pike. Go easy for the first week or so—give their digestive tracks time to adjust to milk and mash as the primary feed, but a few crusts of bread or rotting lettuce will always be well received.

KEEPING THE PEN CLEAN

Your shoats won't be eating (or pooping) too much during these early weeks, but since their shoat pen is likely to be close to home (in the garage or a nearby shed), you want to stay on top of the cleanliness details. I keep a metal wheelbarrow and an old, flat-bottomed shovel near the pen for this task. The shoats will quickly establish one corner of the pen as the primary poop spot, so keep after this with the shovel. Also, gather up any leftover food that they've declined to eat. If there's spoiled bedding, scoop this up, too. Then toss some fresh hay or straw into a corner for them to root around in and go to sleep.

Their pen is never going to smell like a bed of roses, but if you stay on top of the details, it won't ever be too unpleasant. Plus, a clean pen means clean shoats, and clean shoats are more fun to pat and handle. That's your primary goal at this point.

PICKING UP SHOATS

Once your shoats are nicely acclimated and used to your company, it's time to move them out to their permanent quarters. If your shoat pen is inside

Above: Patty the Yorkshire cross explores grass in her new home at Sunrise Farm. It's important to socialize a shoat during its first week on your farm, laying a foundation for working with 300-pound hogs later on.

your main pen, all you need to do is open the gate or dismantle the walls to let them loose. But if the main pen is elsewhere, you'll need to pick up the shoats for transporting them.

Use the partition to crowd the shoats into the corner. (Not having to chase them is always the best way to minimize stress.) Gathering a shoat up in your arms, the way you might a puppy, or the way you might see someone pick up a shoat in the movies, is not the way to go. Shoats are ferocious squirmers, and holding them in your arms will encourage them to redouble their escape efforts. Plus, once you pick one up, it will be squealing as if you'd just slashed it with a knife. The psychological effort of trying to ignore the noise makes it almost impossible to maintain the physical effort of containing four flailing legs and a thrashing snout.

Instead, you should pick up a shoat by grabbing one hind leg. With your hand close to the ground, slowly ease your way over to the shoat. Once you're close enough, swiftly dart your hand out, grab the closest hind leg, and lift straight up. The shoat will squeal and flail, but all of that squealing and flailing will be far from your hand, safely holding onto the one leg as the shoat dangles in space. With nothing to grab or kick for leverage, the shoat will be helpless to escape and safe from injury. Once the initial shock wears off, I usually grab the second hind leg as well to minimize the strain on the one leg. Then set the shoats into their transport box, or whatever you're using, and move them to their summer quarters.

SHOATS AND KIDS

These first few weeks, when the shoats are small and easily contained, is the best time to give children a chance to become familiar with them (and vice versa.) Pigs and children often get along famously because pigs aren't afraid of outstretched hands or unexpected gestures. (Lambs, on the other hand, typically run away from approaching children.) Take the time when your shoats are crowded by the partition to introduce children to the scene.

What typically happens, after a few short moments in which both the pigs and kids stare at one another uncertainly, is that the pigs come over to investigate. They'll snuggle and nip and poke with their noses. The children will rub their backs and try to grab them for cuddling. The pigs will wiggle free. Give the children some bread or food scraps to help lubricate the interaction.

What often happens with time is that the pigs become too aggressive for the kids, biting pants and nipping fingers out of curiosity, not malice. Teach the children to push the pigs' noses away while also reinforcing that the pigs aren't mean, they're just enthusiastic. If the children understand that pigs investigate things with their noses the way we do with our hands, they'll learn not to fear this seemingly aggressive behavior. Soon the shoats and the kids will have fun playing together and look forward to one another's company.

Within a few months, of course, the shoats are going to turn into hogs while the kids are going to remain kids. What started off as rambunctious play could become dangerous for the children as the pigs pass 100 pounds in weight. Make sure not to let children play with or feed adult hogs unattended. (See the subsequent chapters for ways to set up a feeding system that allows children to feed the pigs without having to go into the pen.)

CHAPTER THREE

Where Your Pigs Will Live

Fortunately, a pig is not at all particular in regard to styles of architecture.

—JOSEPH HARRIS

Where will your pigs live? Pretty much anywhere you let them. That's one of the great things about pigs—no muss, no fuss.

That said, you don't want them to live just anywhere. You want them to be happy with where they live. If they're happy, you'll be happy.

If your pigs are happy, they'll also gain weight at a remarkable clip. Is it callous to say in one breath that you want your pigs to live happy lives and in the next that you're hoping their happiness leads to delicious pork chops? No. Consider the alternatives: the "out of sight, out of mind" pork eater acquiesces to pigs being raised in industrial feedlots—very unhappy pigs indeed; and the vegetarian's creed leads to fewer pigs living in the world, happy or otherwise. Neither of these alternatives are particularly attractive if you happen to be a pig.

So the goal of this book, and hopefully your goal as a pig owner, is for there to be lots of pigs, all of them happy.

With that in mind, pig housing can be as simple as a convenient shade tree or as complicated as a full-on building

Opposite: While Tim Sanford does a quick repair to their portable pen, Suzanne Long brings hay for the hogs at Luna Bleu Farm. The movable pen helps the pigs till up fallow vegetable fields.

Above: Gloucestershire Old Spots piglets nap in a pile at North Hollow Farm. The farm has separate areas in the 1886 barn for the pigs to sleep and eat.

with roof, floor, walls, and doors. As long as the pig's basic needs are met, the details are up to you. Here are the things you want to keep in mind as you go about deciding where your pigs will live.

Access to Food and Water

Pigs grow faster—much faster—than any other livestock animal, and that rapid growth is predicated on prodigious quanti-

ties of food and water. Your hands and back will want your pigs to live close by so that you don't have to haul food and water a long distance, especially as the pigs approach maturity, when they will consume about all you can carry. You'll also want to be able to show off your pigs to any visitors and neighborhood kids that stop by, without having to trek a half-mile to do so. Having your pigs close at hand is good.

ODOR

On the other hand, your pigs are going to smell like pigs. Even though great claims are made for pigs' cleanliness and hygienic habits, your nose will be able to detect a whiff of untruth in these claims. How you manage your pigs will have an influence on how much they smell, but nevertheless, you're not going to want them under your kitchen window, as easy as that would make it to toss them the slops.

You want to pick a place that's downwind from your house and not directly upwind from your closest neighbor. Our pigpen is about 50 yards from our house, and unless the wind is blowing directly from them to us, which is rare, we don't smell them. (And even then, it's just an occasional whiff.) We run a length of plastic hose out from the house faucet to a valve by the pen, which takes care of toting the water. A few 5-gallon plastic buckets (or, in times of surplus, a wheelbarrow) handle the food chores quite easily.

SHADE

Your pigs will very much like some shade through the hot part of the summer, both for protection from sunburn and from overheating. If you're planning a nice, solid roof over their heads, that will work fine. If not, overhanging trees and shrubs are excellent, especially if the branches overhang the pen while the trunks remain outside, since the pigs will work on the bark all summer and possibly damage the tree's trunk and roots. Another shade option is to simply string a durable tarp between several trees to cast a shadow.

Shade is crucial for porcine happiness, especially for the pink-skinned breeds like the Yorkshire. The first year we had pigs, I hadn't finished building their pen yet, so upon bringing the shoats home, I put them into an idle sheep pen inside the barn. I left the door to the outside open, assuming the little guys would go running outside to explore. I was wrong. After several days, they still hadn't; they were pink little Yorkshire crosses who had been born in a barn and had never been outside in their lives.

On day three, I used a scrap piece of plywood to corral them over by the door, slowly easing them out into the sunlight as they screamed bloody murder. Once outside, they stood frozen in place for several minutes, apparently paralyzed in fear. Then one of them grunted. Another one grunted in response. They all put their noses down, cut a few furrows in the barnyard dirt, and immediately realized the benefits of life out-of-doors. Off they went, snuffling around the barnyard.

The next day was sunny, and the shoats were outside all day until midafternoon. When I went to check on them, I noticed that their ears were scorched red from the sun. I rounded up two friends and more plywood scraps to push them back into the barn, but the damage had been done: their poor ears soon blistered and peeled. After that experience, I've been sure to introduce pink-skinned piglets to the sunshine as gradually as possible, either by limiting their exposure for the first few days or by putting them in a pen that's mostly shaded. After a few weeks, they seem both smarter and toughened enough to handle sun on their own.

WARMTH

Pigs are pretty rugged creatures, but in the cold days of spring and autumn, they'd prefer to have some dry, solid ground under foot for rooting and bedding. The first year we raised pigs (those same poor pigs!), the early autumn

Above: Louise the Tamworth sow eats hay on a sunny winter morning at Hogwash Farm. The farm uses Port-A-Hut enclosures, which can shelter four pigs on cold winter nights.

weather turned out to be cold (with temperatures in the 30s and 40s) and rainy. The pigpen that had worked well all summer turned into soup, and though I strung a tarp across somewhat higher ground to provide a place for the pigs to crawl out of the mud, they suffered. They didn't end up weighing as much as their brethren the following year, who came from the breeder at roughly the same time of year. Since then, I've extended the pen to include some higher ground and made sure that the tarp keeps off rain as well as sun. Pigs will happily slog around in mud and muck, especially on warm days, but they'd much rather sleep on dry ground or bedding, out of the rain. Contented pigs are what you're after.

Moisture

At the same time, during the hot days of summer, your pigs will love nothing more than a low, wet spot for rolling in the mud to cool off. The ideal pigpen includes both high ground for wet weather and low ground for dry weather, when some soft, spongy ground will be perfect for midsummer lolling. If your wet spot gets too dry, you can always augment the wallow with your garden hose, assuming your water supply is sufficient.

Pasture

Finally, your pigs will love to have some access to pasture, either of the green, grassy kind or that of the open woodland. Pigs live for furrowing their noses through dirt and sod and grass and muck of all kinds. "Pasture-raised pork" is all the rage these days, and even though it's something of a misnomer to compare pasture-raised pork with pasture-raised beef or lamb (where the animals eat pasture exclusively), the implication of pasture-raised pork is that the pigs who produced it were having a good time and enjoying life.

As you can see, when it comes to where your pigs will live, there is a balance to be struck: close yet not too close, dry yet not too dry, warm yet not too warm. No single spot on your land is likely to meet all these criteria perfectly, so you'll need to pick and choose to work with what you have. If that includes big fields and a tractor, moving food and water to distant pastures may be no big deal. If you have a great mucky spot with no high ground, build a pig house with a floor that allows the animals to walk inside when they want to be warm and dry. If you have pasture with no shade, build a roof. You get the idea.

One thing you should know about where your pigs live: They're going to transform it into dirt and mud. Completely. (Unless the pen is huge—acres in size.) Our original pigpen was under a tree island (in the middle of a pasture) that used to be a sylvan glade of sorts, with lots of ferns and undergrowth. Now it looks like the area in front of the soccer goal on a busy middle-school playground. If, in the future, you decide to stop raising pigs or to house them elsewhere, you can always seed the pen back to grass

and legumes. But in the meantime, it's going to be a mud bowl.

PUTTING A ROOF OVER THEIR HEADS

Another wonderful attribute of pigs is that they can make do with all sorts of jury-rigged shelters that the more self-respecting livestock (horses come immediately to mind) would consider substandard. There are as many solutions to the pig-shelter question as there are people raising pigs.

As I mentioned previously, a sturdy tarp strung between trees can be all the shelter you need to provide, assuming that it's covering high ground where the pigs can get out of the rain and muck if needed. Another year, our pigs lived underneath an old tree house that had been attached to the side of a pine tree about 6 feet off the ground. That was a very easy solution, though rain blew under the open sides during heavy storms.

Some folks use old garden sheds or metal outbuildings, with any fragile or delicate fittings removed. The pigs are going to scratch and rub against

Above: A Tamworth hog roams near a pig penthouse built with salvaged building materials at Sunrise Farm. Shade is crucial to porcine happiness.

their shelter, so it needs to be relatively strong. The pigs won't go at it maliciously, unless it's the only interesting object available to them in a too small and boring pen, but they will go at it from time to time.

I've seen folks use old steel culverts (the big kind—4 feet or more in diameter) as shelter, being sure that the culvert is staked down so that it can't roll around and injure the pigs.

There are also small, Quonset-shaped metal shelters that are designed specifically for pigs. Since the roof and walls are metal, there are few corners and weak spots for the pigs to push against. Check the Internet for ideas, photographs, and suppliers: One of our neighbors has had good luck with shelters bought from www.port-a-hut.com.

Other folks just nail a few sheets of plywood together to form a teepee shape and call it good. These work well for piglets but not so well for hogs, unless the shelter is strengthened with dimensional lumber and screws. A variation on this is to stand a bunch of pallets on end, drive stakes down into the ground to hold them in place, and stretch a tarp or pieces of metal roofing across the top. Voilà!

One year, I had some leftover metal roofing on hand from an old, collapsed shed. I took a piece of 4x8, ¾-inch plywood, put some 2x6 joists underneath, built walls 2 feet high on the short sides, and brought the roofing together to form an A-frame about 4 feet tall in the middle. I left one long side mostly open for a door and closed the other side in. It sleeps three hogs comfortably, four in a pinch (assuming the first three will let the fourth in). Friends of mine splashed up the walls with paint, creating a very posh porcine penthouse.

The best part of visiting other people who raise pigs is seeing what they've done for shelter. No two solutions are alike, and everyone's improvisation seems to lead in new directions. I've heard of a guy a few towns over who removed the seats from a school bus, put the whole thing on blocks, built a ramp up to the back door, and called it good. Those must be some pretty well-schooled pigs by now.

 Above: With an assist from friends (not pictured) and his dog, Olive, the author uses his tractor to move a portable pen he built to house his hogs at Sunrise Farm.

How Much Space per Pig?

This brings up the question of how much shelter space to provide per pig. I've found that 10 square feet per animal will be required as your hogs reach maturity. (This is just the

shelter space, mind you, meaning the area under the roof.) Pigs don't need space for moving around and setting up house—they're going to sleep one against another for companionship no matter how big the space is. The extra space is more to make sure that the animals can move past one another without creating undue friction or hostility. If your shelter has a doorway, make sure it's wide enough so that one or two pigs can't monopolize it to keep the others out.

One year, I had four hogs sharing the abovementioned shelter that was built atop a sheet of 4x8 plywood. (This amounted to only 8 square feet per animal.) All was fine until the hogs topped the 250-pound mark, when the quarters became cramped. The first three animals would go inside and block the door against the fourth, who would have to push and shove to gain admittance. This would often lead to a fourth-and-goal situation, with the odd hog out running full tilt into the doorway like a football linebacker, scrambling up and over the blocking bodies before rolling down the other side onto the straw-lined floor. This was fun for me to watch but much less fun, I'm sure, for the stressed-out animal who didn't want to sleep outside, alone.

A final note: If your shelter is large enough to contain your fully grown hogs, it's going to be too large for containing the shoats when they're newly arrived. The shoats are likely to designate one side for sleeping and the other for pooping, which is apt to lead to very smelly quarters. The solution is to build a temporary partition to limit the animals to one section of the shelter when they're still small. They won't poop in their own beds and instead will be trained to poop outside. After the shoats grow into hogs, just remove the partition.

THE PORTABLE PEN

As you can see, there are endless solutions to the question of where your pigs will live. Here's yet another: the portable pen.

Not long ago, I read an article in *Small Farmer's Journal* about some organic-pork producers in Maine who raised their animals in portable pens, using a small tractor to tow the pens to fresh ground every now and again. I was intrigued and built myself such a pen the following spring. It's 8 feet by 16 feet in size, with one half contained by walls and a roof and the other half open to the sky and surrounded by metal "hog panels"—those welded-wire pieces of fence that are strong enough to withstand porcine investigation.

Opposite: After the portable pen was moved to new ground, a hog immediately began rooting the fresh pasture, turning the dirt and leaving nutrients behind.

Above: Louisa, six, and Silas Monahan, eight, of Cambridge, MA, keep an eye on the hogs as the author feeds them radicchio leaves in their portable pen. The Monahan family spends summers on the farm, with the kids helping to feed the pigs and harvest vegetables.

The advantages of this system are numerous. The pigs have regular access to sod and fresh ground, which they absolutely adore. The smell is kept to a minimum because the poop is left behind before it can start to pile up. The left-behind poop, of course,

becomes great fertilizer once incorporated back into the soil. The pigs become very tame and sociable because it's easy for you to lean into the pen to scratch their ears; visitors also like the system because there's no electric fencing to worry about. Also, when you need to catch your pigs (either for a de-worming or for slaughter), you don't have to struggle—the pigs are already caught. Finally, if you want to use your portable pen as a simple shelter, you can always park the thing, remove the free end, and run some electric fencing to make a fixed pen. Now you have a nice shelter and corral, all in one.

The disadvantages of the portable shelter are two: The shelter is heavy enough that you really need a tractor or all-terrain vehicle or four-wheel-drive pickup truck (or perhaps a half-dozen strong friends) to move it; and the ground that gets left behind after the pen has moved will be very inviting to your family dog. These disadvantages can be ameliorated somewhat— you can make the shelter lighter and you can throw grass seed down or rototill behind the pen as you go— but they are still disadvantages.

Nevertheless, the advantages of the portable pen are so great that I plan to move entirely in that direction over the next few years. Pasture-raised pork is the ultimate pork. Unless you can fence your pigs onto fresh pasture each year, and somehow arrange the fencing and feeding and shelter accordingly, you're limited in your access to pasture over time. With the portable pen, these problems are solved.

The majority of all the protein that your pigs eat in the course of their six-month-long lives ends up not in their meat but in their manure. That's why the industrial hog-raising business faces such a pollution problem—pig poop is very rich in nitrogen. Raising your hogs in a portable pen allows you to capture this fertility and put it to good use instead of creating pollution. Between the manure and the rototilling action of the pigs, some people refer to these pens as "pig tractors," since the end result of the pen's passage is similar to a field prepared for seeding.

The pen I made is a modification of the model I saw in *Small Farmer's Journal* (which was only a photo, after all), and you should feel free to modify it to your own needs. The key is that it needs to rest on skids for towing and that it needs to be braced enough to withstand both moving and porcine scratching.

I made mine from rough-cut hemlock that my neighbor saws in abundance, meaning that the 2x6 lumber is a true 2 inches by 6 inches. Using kiln-dried lumber from a store would also work, though you'd have to adjust the following dimensions slightly.

BUILDING THE PORTABLE PEN

Materials needed:

1x4 by 10 feet: 6
2x4 by 8 feet: 5
2x4 by 10 feet: 5
2x6 by 8 feet: 12
2x6 by 10 feet: 4
2x6 by 12 feet: 1
2x6 by 16 feet: 2
$5/8$-inch rough plywood: 3 sheets
Hog panels: 34 inches by 8 feet: 3
$1/2$-inch by 5-inch carriage bolts with nuts: 4
Fencing staples for attaching hog panels: several pounds
Roofing: either three sheets of 36-inch-by-10-foot metal, or
 possibly a tarp
Miscellaneous screws or nails, for attaching the dimensional
 lumber together and for attaching the plywood to the framing

- **Step One: Building the Back Wall.** Take two 2x6x8s and lay them on a flat surface, parallel, about 4 feet apart, standing up on their 2-inch sides. Cut five pieces, 44 inches long, out of three of the other 2x6x8s. Arrange these five pieces between the two 8s such that two of them are at the outsides, one is in the middle, and the other two are evenly spaced in between, all standing on their 2-inch sides. Nail or screw all of these together to create a framing wall, and nail or screw a sheet of plywood across the whole works, squaring up the wall as you do so. This is the back wall.

- **Step Two: Attaching the Back Wall.** Lay your two 2x8x16-foot skids, 8 feet apart (outside to outside dimension) on a flat surface. (Note: Make sure you do this in a place where you'll be able to drive your tractor or truck later on to move the finished structure.) These should be resting on their 6-inch faces, like skids. Place the back wall on top of one end of the skids, with the plywood facing out and flush with the ends of the skids, and attach it to the skids.

- **Step Three: Building the Front Wall.** Cut two 2x6x8s to 7 feet 3 and ⅜ inches and attach them to the skids, laying them flat, one on top of each skid, and butting them up against the back wall. Now cut the 2x6x12 in half, and attach each 6-foot piece vertically so that it stands in front of (and butted up against) the doubled skid plate. The distance from the outside edge of the back wall plywood to the front edge of these vertical posts should be 8 feet exactly. Cut two more 2x6x8s to exactly 8 feet, and nail one between the bottom of the vertical posts and one across the top of the vertical posts to create the front wall.

- **Step Four: Bracing the Front Wall.** Install diagonal corner braces on this front wall to give the building rigidity. Square the front wall up, and mark in 30 inches from the inside of each vertical post, along the top 2x6x8. Stand a 2x4x8 up next to the vertical post, and then angle the top out to the 30-inch line. Mark the 2x4 to length so that it's flush with both top and bottom 2x6s, cut, and attach. Repeat on the other side.

- **Step Five: Installing the Rafters.** Lay the five 2x4x10s across between the front and back walls, with an even overhang on each end. Notch them slightly so that they sit well on the two wall plates, and cut the fronts at an angle to make them perpendicular to the ground. Space these rafters evenly across the roof, with one placed above each side wall (flush to the outside), one in the middle, and the other two splitting the difference. Attach them all around.

- **Step Six: Building the Side Walls.** Using the 2x6x10s, cut four vertical studs for each wall. Place one stud right up against the back wall, and the other three evenly spaced between the front and back walls. Hold them up against the rafter and mark before cutting to length. Notch each stud so that it sits with its outside face flush with each rafter and with the bottom skids. Attach all around. Then square everything up and attach a plywood sheet to each side, making sure that the bottom edge of the plywood is flush with the top of the 16-foot skids (and even with the bottom edge of the back wall).

- **Step Seven: Building the Free-End Wall.** Take two of the 2x6x8s and attach them to an 8-foot hog panel so that they are flush with the top and bottom of the panel. Nail them on using heavy fencing staples.

- **Step Eight: Building the Free-End Posts.** Cut a 2x6x8 into two 34-inch sections. Cut a 2x4x8 into two 30-inch sections. Join one 2x4 section to one 2x6 section in an L shape, so that the 2-inch face of the 2x4 is flat against one edge of a 6-inch face of a 2x6. Keep the butt ends flush so that the 2x4 is 4 inches shorter than the 2x6. Repeat with the other side, aligning the pieces so that they are the mirror image of the first.

- **Step Nine: Building the Hog-Panel Walls.** Install the free-end posts to the far end of the 2x6 skids such that the 2x6 side of the post is facing away from the shelter and the 2x4 sides are facing one another. Cut two 2x4x8s to 7 feet 10 inches, and install them between the free-end posts and the shelter front wall so that they serve as top rails. The free-end side will sit atop the 2x4. Screw through the 2x6 on the shelter-wall side to hold the rails in place, parallel to the skid. Now attach the 8-foot hog panels to the insides of these walls, using fencing staples. The panels should exactly fit.

- **Step Ten: Attaching the Free-End Wall.** Using a ⅝-inch drill, bore holes through the free-end wall and the free-end posts so that you can slide the ½-inch bolts through the four corners of the wall. Attach the wall using the bolts, placing the nuts on the outside, away from the pigs.

- **Step Eleven: Attaching the Roof.** Strap the roof with the 1x4x10s, cutting each piece to 9 feet long and spacing them evenly across the rafters. Attach the three 10-foot pieces of metal roofing using gasket screws.

That's it—not so bad. Use your spare lumber to build a feeder that you can hang from one of the hog panels, close to the ground. It will slide along with the shelter as you move it. If you're looking to save money and weight, you can skip the metal roof and just stretch a tarp across the rafters, removing it in winter if you live in an area where snow piles up. If you have lots of scrap lumber lying around, you can also skip the plywood and use your scraps for the walls. If you're willing to live dangerously, you could downscale the pen and use 2x4 lumber all around, though I'm not convinced it would hold up well over time. You'll be on your own.

CHAPTER FOUR

What Your Pigs Will Eat

The hog is a great eater. He can eat, and digest, and assimilate, more nutriment in a given time, in proportion to his size, than any other of our domestic animals.

—JOSEPH HARRIS

No single moment in farm life is quite as delightful as feeding a bunch of hungry pigs. Down go the slops with a satisfying flop. Up steam the pigs, grunting and squeaking in delight. Immediately the battle is engaged. Snorting, snacking, smacking, the pigs bulldoze through the pile, finding the sweetest, squishiest parts to eat first. Nobody ever told pigs to chew with their mouths closed, so they don't, chomping away in unselfconscious glee, a large percentage of the food finding its way into stomachs but a still-substantial amount dripping down jowls and cheeks, to be snuffled up on the next pass. Before long, the trough cleared, their work done, victory ensured, the pigs trundle off to a shady corner and arrange themselves in an impromptu pile, to sleep it off and gather strength for the next feeding.

Pigs are omnivores, which is the fundamental detail to know about pigs. None of our other livestock companions are. Sure, chickens eat a pretty wide range of stuff, and horses will go for everything from a sugar cube to an apple to a bag of oats, but that pales in

Opposite: While she eats, Flo has her ears scratched by Tim Sanford. Flo is one of two sows that Sanford and Suzanne Long keep for breeding at Luna Bleu Farm.

comparison to the pig, who will eat almost anything, at least once, from grubs and roots to fruits and vegetables to chickens and, if the unlikely situation presented itself, probably horseflesh, too.

The usefulness of this trait is undoubtedly what led pigs to be among the very first animals domesticated by humans back at the dawn of agriculture. Pigs eat everything we eat, which makes them perfectly situated for eating our leftovers. They also eat a lot of stuff that we don't, including spoiled milk, rotten fruit, and raw grains. They were an indispensable part of the self-sufficient farms of old, turning stuff that we humans couldn't eat into something that we very much could and did: pork. Pigs are the original alchemists, transforming dross into gold.

The pig's omnivory is also why the pig is so smart. Or, stated in a way that is less pejorative to the rest of the animal kingdom, why the pig's brain works so much like ours, another dominant omnivore. Omnivory implies choice, and choice requires thought. Omnivores can eat almost anything, including new sources of food that suddenly become available, allowing the omnivore to flourish in a wide range of ever-changing conditions. Yet such an expansive appetite also increases the risk of eating something harmful or lethal. Omnivory, therefore, necessitates attention to detail, careful selection, the ability to evaluate new situations, and a formidable memory.

No wonder that pigs are the escape artists of the farm. In the off moments when food is not at the top of their list, they turn their substantial intelligence to understanding fences and gates.

The pig's omnivory also explains why eating pork has been problematic in human history and why pork is singled out from among all meats for repeated restrictions and prohibitions in ancient religious texts. Because the pig's appetite and digestive tract is similar to ours, it follows that many of the nasty bugs, germs, and viruses that plague humans also plague pigs. Accidentally ingesting a touch of cow flop or a sheep pellet isn't likely to make you sick, especially if these herbivores have been grazing on grass. Accidentally ingesting some pig poop, however, is another story; their germs are our germs. With proper farming and slaughter methods, how-

Above: The Andrews sisters—three Yorkshire cross pigs—dine on grain and garden scraps held in a stout trough built by the author at Sunrise Farm.

ever, we humans have used our own omnivorous intelligence to figure out how to safely handle pork.

But back to the front end of the pig. What is the best way to go about feeding a pig?

BUILDING A PIG TROUGH

The easiest way to get food to pigs is to build a simple trough to hold the food. Such a trough isn't strictly required, since pigs will gladly snuffle their food right off the ground if needed, and since they will undoubtedly shovel a bunch of the food out of the trough and onto the ground anyway. But a trough is a nice way to contain more expensive food, like grain, and to contain the debris somewhat.

To build a stout, portable trough that your pigs can easily access yet have trouble flipping over, and that will be relatively easy for you to clean and manage, lay your hands on two 2x8s, one 2x6, and two 2x4s. Eight-footers will work for up to five pigs, since you'll want to allow about a foot and a half of trough length per pig.

Let's say you have three pigs. Cut one of the 2x6s and one of the 2x8s to 4 feet 6 inches (1.5 feet per pig times 3 pigs). Screw the 2x6 into the 2x8 to create a long, v-shaped channel; do this by laying the 2x6 flat on the ground, standing the 2x8 up next to it, and screwing through the 2x8 into the 2x6. Cut two 3-foot sections out of the other 2x8, and screw these sections into either end of your v-shaped channel to create perpendicular ends. (Hold the v slightly off the ground so that the tops of the v are flush with the top of the end.) Finally, cut your 2x4s to 4 feet 9 inches and screw them down to either side of the v and the tops of the legs. These will make the v somewhat deeper and also help attach the v to the legs.

For extra credit, cut your extra 2x4 sections into short pieces that will just fit across the trough from side to side. Screw one of these crosspieces in about a foot and a half from either end. These braces will further strengthen the trough (which is already quite pig-proof) and also deter any one of the pigs from lying in the trough during feeding time, effectively monopolizing the entire food supply and keeping the others from eating.

WHERE TO PUT THE PIG TROUGH

Where you locate your pig trough will have a major impact on your life while the pigs are in residence. You'll be feeding them twice per day for five or six months. On some days, you'll have lots of time to spend with the animals and will probably be wearing sturdy rubber boots and old clothes. In this case, the trough can be anywhere inside their fence. But on other days, you'll remember to feed the pigs just before heading into town to do errands and you'll be wearing clean clothes and street shoes. For these occasions, you'll want to be able to fill the trough without stepping into the enclosure.

In my discussion of fencing in chapter 5, I recommend using mostly electric fence to create your pig enclosure, with the exception of around the feeding area, where a wooden fence has many advantages. Chief among these is that you can attach the trough directly to the wooden fence, where you can easily pour food into the trough without getting your feet muddy in the pen. In this scenario, modify your trough somewhat so that you can attach one of the long sides directly to the fence with heavy screws. Then drive a metal stake into the ground at the end of each leg (and secure it to the leg) to keep the pigs from levering the trough off of the fence. Your pigs are going to spend a lot of time pushing and heaving and prying against the trough, and if it isn't securely attached to the fence, they will eventually rip it off and flip it over. This will defeat the purpose of being able to keep yourself clean during feeding time as you tiptoe into the pen, trying to right the trough before the pigs rub against your clean pants.

The final consideration in trough placement is to choose relatively high and dry ground for the feeding area. The first year we had pigs, I placed the trough in a low, wettish spot, figuring that pigs would like the soft earth. By the time a rainy autumn settled in, the pigs could scarcely reach the trough through the oozing mud, which came up to their bellies and beyond. I'm convinced they ended up eating less food than the subsequent years' pigs because of their reluctance to brave the swamp around the trough.

WHAT TO PUT IN THE PIG TROUGH

Some people feed their pigs nothing but vegetable scraps and gleanings from the garden all summer. Others materialize with pickup trucks full of stale bread and spoiled goods from the local bakery. Some feed special grain mixes designed for optimal weight gain. Others forage the land for dropped apples and anything remotely resembling food. As I mentioned, pigs will eat almost anything, at least once.

Above: Nancy LaRowe at Hogwash Farm feeds her pigs produce and stale bagels that she occasionally picks up from a local food cooperative. LaRowe gives her pigs a consistent diet, supplementing it with treats from the market.

Here's where a little cost-benefit analysis comes in handy. Your ultimate goal in raising pigs, besides the companionship and humor that comes from having pigs on the property, is pork. And in most cases, investing in a little quality pig food can more than pay for itself down the road in quality pork.

I had one friend, the manager of a rustic mountain lodge, who borrowed two pigs from a local farmer for the summer. He figured it would be fun to have a few pigs on hand for the

overnight guests to see, plus he planned to feed the kitchen-prep scraps to the pigs instead of paying to have them taken to the dump. All went well until the fall date came when the lodge closed for the winter and the pigs went back down the hill to their original farm for final fattening before slaughter. The two pigs turned out to be roughly half the size of their littermates, who had spent the summer on the farm. Even though my friend thought he had been feeding them amply all summer, the farmer's question, upon seeing the returning pigs, was, "What've you been feeding them up there, the thin air?"

Feeding pigs nothing but high-end, store-bought grain can reduce your pork profit margin somewhat. But feeding them nothing but gleaned vegetables can end up doing the same. My recommendation is that you feed some amount of good grain every day, which will ensure a balanced, healthy diet. As a friend of mine says, "You feed pigs to make money, not to save money." In other words, the best feed leads to the best pork; scrimping on feed will reduce the quality and quantity (and price per pound) of your finished product.

Most feed stores sell 50-pound bags of grain that have been specially blended for pigs. Many brands come in two varieties: medicated and non-medicated. Check the bag's label to be sure you're getting the non-medicated stuff. (If antibiotic-laced pork is what you're after, save yourself the trouble and buy it for cheap at the supermarket.) Store the feed at your

place in metal or plastic trash cans to keep any rodents at bay. Keep in mind that three hogs approaching market weight will be eating close to a bag of grain each day. Since big trash cans hold three bags, you might want to buy several cans to get you through a week.

When you do feed grain, soak it in water for 30 seconds or so before adding it to the trough. I usually feed grain to my pigs using a 5-gallon bucket, scooping in the grain first and then adding water until it fills to the level of the grain. The water softens the grain somewhat, makes it more palatable, and helps ensure that the pigs are getting enough water. They clearly like soaked grain more than dry grain; I figured this out after realizing that the pigs always cleared the trough on rainy days, when the grain became soft and squishy.

With good grain as the basis of the diet, augment it with as much free stuff as you can lay your hands on. Baked goods provide lots of carbohydrates and fat and tend to lead to voluptuous pigs, especially suitable for bacon. Vegetables tend to be eaten with less gusto, and since they contain fewer calories than baked goods, lead to leaner pork in the end. Keep in mind that pig fat will retain some of the flavor of the food that's fed to it—that's why pork from European pigs raised exclusively on white oak acorns can fetch upward of $100 per pound. On the flip side, feeding your pigs primarily moldy jelly donuts is apt to lead to a disappointing product. As the saying goes: Junk in, junk out.

My favorite free pig food is apples, especially drops, which are available in abundance in Vermont from late summer through autumn in many backyards and side pastures. I grind the apples in a small cider press that we have and let them soften and ferment slightly before feeding them. At that point stand clear of the trough; the pigs charge the apple mash, snuffling up whatever grain and vegetables happen to get in their way. There's nothing more satisfying than watching a satisfied pig. Or tastier than apple-finished pork.

WHAT *NOT* TO PUT IN THE PIG TROUGH

Even though pigs will eat almost anything, they shouldn't be allowed to. Here's what you should never feed your pigs: meat scraps, either from farm animals or wildlife, or any uncooked, commercial plate waste or table scraps.

The pigs' greatest benefit—its ability to eat exactly what we do, and more—is also its greatest danger to us humans. As mentioned, many of the parasites and diseases that affect us also affect them. The easiest way to pass these parasites and diseases back and forth between us is through food.

Chief among these dangers are the parasitic nematodes of the Trichinae family, whose larva lead to trichinosis (and all those prohibitions against eating pork down through the ages). Trichinae nematodes lay their eggs in the flesh of a variety of carnivores and omnivores, including both pigs and humans. Eating raw or under-cooked pork that is infected with the nematodes will deliver the worms straight into the human body. Hence the simple advice: Don't feed meat to pigs. No meat, no nematodes; no nematodes, no risk of infection.

A variation on this "no meat" theme is don't put your pigs in a position to eat wildlife, either, because wild animals can be infected with Trichinae worms, especially skunks, raccoons, and possums. More than likely, your sty or electric fence will keep these critters away from your pigs. Don't nullify this advantage by throwing fresh roadkill to your pigs under the theory that "they'll eat anything." They will. This is not what you want.

The final "no meat" variation is to prevent your pigs from catching and eating rodents, who also can carry Trichinae worms. Make sure that your grain is stored in a rodent-proof container so that you aren't chumming rats and mice into your pig area. Also, clean up around your pig feeder every now and again to make sure that undesirable leftovers aren't festering in a corner, attracting rodents. You needn't be 100 percent fastidious—rodents aren't easy to catch, even for quick-footed pigs. You just don't want the pigpen to be teeming with rats and mice.

Uncooked garbage and table scraps can also be vectors for a whole host of bacteria and viruses that humans and pigs share in common, not least of which is the infamous "swine flu." The way to ensure that we're not passing illness back and forth is not to pass any common food back and forth. If you want to feed restaurant scraps to your pigs, you must first boil the

Above: Three of the Tamworths called the Gang of Four eat their morning helping of grain at Sunrise Farm. Soaking grain in water for a minute or two not only makes the grain more palatable for the pigs but also ensures they're getting enough water.

scraps for thirty minutes before feeding. That's the law. Since most people don't have the desire or facilities to be reheating garbage, it's easier to avoid the problem altogether and send the table scraps to the compost heap instead.

Now here's the good news: If you follow these two rules—no meat and no table scraps—you're entirely in the clear. You could probably eat your pork raw without any danger (not that I'm recommending that). But there's no reason to feel any more fear or trepidation about pork than about any other meat, provided you follow the "no meat, no table scraps" rules.

Still not convinced? Laws prohibiting the feeding of table scraps to pigs only date back to the 1950s in the United States. For most of us, then, our parents and grandparents grew up having a justifiable fear of getting trichinosis from undercooked pork, and they transferred this fear to us. But times have changed—in this case, for the better.

HOW MUCH TO FEED

Your ideal each day is to feed your pigs exactly as much as they can finish after putting in a Herculean effort. Feed them less than this, and you're missing a chance to put some more weight on them. Feed them more than this, and you're just wasting food (and, potentially, attracting mice and rodents to do the cleanup work). I try to gauge my feeding so that the trough is more or less empty before the next feeding, with it being completely empty (and the area around the trough, therefore, scoured clean by the pigs) every few days. If the trough always has something in it, you're just conditioning your pigs to eat with less urgency and efficiency.

Officially, growing pigs are said to eat between 2 and 8 pounds of food per day, though I've never bothered with a scale and wouldn't want to limit them based on theory. Some food always ends up trampled or spilled from the trough. I try to stick to the "trough completely clean every few days" approach and make adjustments accordingly.

I find that changes in the weather will affect how much the pigs eat. Very hot, humid weather leads to porcine lethargy and less food consumption. Cool autumn evenings seem to fire the appetite. I have the notion that my pigs eat more when the barometer is falling—stocking up on calories before the storm hits—but I may be imagining that.

One thing that I'm not imagining is the importance of regularity in feeding. Set a schedule for when you feed your pigs and try to stick to it as much as you can. The pigs will anticipate it and not get stressed wondering when the next feeding is coming along. Occasional lapses are fine—I've even double-fed pigs in the morning when I know I'm going to be away that same night—but as exceptions, not the rule.

In general I find that pigs like to sleep late in the morning and don't like to eat at night. (Contrast that with sheep, who are reliably up at the crack of dawn and will even feed all night, especially when there's a moon.) I aim to feed my pigs between 7 AM and 8 AM in the morning and between 5 PM and 6 PM at night, all things being equal. Especially when the cooler mornings of autumn arrive, the pigs will still be sacked out at 8 AM, meaning that I get to watch them wake up as I arrive with the food. There's no funnier sight than pigs waking up. They crack an eye, they think about it, they squirm around a bit, they slowly stand up, stretch a leg or two, and if I'm especially lucky, they yawn.

Pigs yawn with all the disregard and idleness of the typical American teenager on a Saturday morning. They open right up—give it a good, solid effort—while staring off into the middle distance, gathering their thoughts for the day. They say that yawns are contagious, and though I can't say that I've ever caught a yawn from my pigs, I've certainly wanted to. They make the yawn seem like one of life's essential pleasures, to be drawn out and savored, never rushed.

Finally, another way to go is to make or buy a self-feeder and let the pigs decide how much to eat and when. I haven't tried this approach, both because the feeders aren't cheap and because they are limited to dispensing clean, dry grain. Try feeding wet grain, or grain mixed with apple mash, and the mechanism will clog right up. I'm also around on our farm every day during hog-raising season (or one of my friends or farmhands is), so I haven't felt the compulsion to set up a feeding system that would work while I'm gone.

WATER

The last thing to consider when feeding pigs is that they need a constant supply of clean water. This is not quite as easy as it sounds.

Any bucket, pail, trough, or puddle of water will inevitably inspire your pigs to put at least one leg into it, luxuriating in the liquid while they slurp it down. Small pails and troughs are also perfect playthings and will end up flipped over in a pool of mud at the slightest provocation. Then there's always the jockeying for best position at the water trough, which quickly leads to an overturned mess.

Meanwhile, if they don't get enough water, your pigs will respond by eating less. This works against your goal of happy pigs and copious pork.

There are a number of solutions to the water problem. The first—one that our farm does not enjoy the benefit of—is a nearby, all-season brook. Run a pipe from the brook into a small stock tank, and your work is done. The pigs will still muddy the waters from time to time, but the steady inflow of fresh water will keep things clean and nice.

I've done my best to emulate the babbling brook by running a garden hose to a 25-gallon, low-lying plastic stock tank that I half-tuck under the electric fence. The 25 gallons is more than they will drink between feedings, and the hot fence running across the middle prevents them from stepping into the tank for a bath. When I arrive with the slops, I turn on the hose and let it run. After five or ten minutes of laying out the food and scratching all the ears and rumps within easy reach, I turn the hose back off. The excess flow helps keep the water clear and also creates a nice mud hole downstream from the tank.

An even simpler solution, especially when the pigs are young, is to use an ordinary 5-gallon rubber animal pail, available at feed stores everywhere. These are easy to tip over and rinse out between fillings, and I find that the shoats generally don't tip them over for the first month. After that, however, keeping the rubber pail from turning into a toy is all but impossible.

Opposite: Waking up from a morning nap, one of the piglets at Luna Bleu Farm lets a good yawn rip. Pigs make yawns seem like one of life's essential pleasures.

Above: Patty the Yorkshire cross uses the water bucket for drinking and a quick cool-down at Sunrise Farm.

A longer-term solution for larger pigs is to hang a bucket to the side of your wooden fence section. Do this in such a way that you can still dump the bucket out from time to time. I'd recommend attaching the bucket using baling twine or wire so that you can pivot the bucket to clean out any debris that might fall in. Five-gallon buckets are useful for this task, though they are too deep for a hog's head to reach the bottom. Provided you have a hose near at hand for refilling, pouring out the leftover water is no big deal.

Opposite: Chi Chi, a Large Black and Tamworth sow, drinks water on a sunny winter morning at Hogwash Farm. During the colder months, the pigs are kept closer to the barn for easy access to water.

Above: Oreo Cookie drinks from a bucket of water outfitted with water nipples at Sunrise Farm. Water nipples are handy, especially when water needs to be carried a long distance to the pen.

USING WATER NIPPLES

If you don't have a hose at hand and will therefore be hauling water some distance to your pigs, you might want to consider buying metal pig-watering nipples. These reduce waste and excess spillage altogether because they only release water when the pig is biting down on the nipple and drinking. If your pigs are spilling 3 gallons of water twice per day, you'll be carrying an extra 3 to 4 tons of water over the course of the summer—something to be avoided!

Pig-watering nipples cost about $5 apiece and come in two versions, one for shoats and one for hogs. I usually give water to my shoats in a rubber water pail, so I only need to buy the hog nipples and make the switch once the animals reach two months of age or so.

The nipples come threaded and ready for installation. Buy a set of rubber washers, metal washers, and a ½-inch pipe fitting for each nipple—three nipples will be perfect for a 5-gallon bucket, which will keep three pigs happy. Drill a hole for each nipple about an inch up from the bottom of the bucket (basically as close as you can to the bottom of the bucket while leaving enough space for your fingers to install the washers and nut on the inside of the bucket). Space the three nipples about 60 degrees apart. This will leave more than half of the bucket's circumference untouched so that you can hang it against your wooden fence section or the wall of your shelter.

How high to place the bucket? The pigs will be most happy if the nipples are right at snout level. Higher than this, and they will have trouble reaching it. Lower than this, and they will have trouble sucking the water uphill into their mouths, spilling lots of it on the ground. If you've hung the bucket on wire or twine, raise it up every few weeks as the pigs grow.

CHAPTER FIVE

Fencing

Ordinary farm men have been so accustomed to let pigs wallow in the mire, and take care of themselves, that it is very difficult to get them to realize the importance of cleanliness, regularity in feeding, general kindness, and constant attention.

—JOSEPH HARRIS

Fencing is the heart of the matter when it comes to raising pigs. The decisions you make about how to fence your pigs will affect almost every other aspect of their lives with you—how you feed and care for them, how much fun they have with you, how much fun you have with them, how easy or hard it is to handle them, and, ultimately, how their lives will come to an end. Before you make any other decision about your overall pig management strategy, therefore, I recommend you read this chapter and craft your own approach to fencing.

HOW BIG SHOULD A PIGPEN BE?

From the pigs' perspective, there is no upper limit. Feral pigs roam over territories that extend to square miles. Pigs live for their noses, and their noses live for excitement and novelty as well as for the familiar and the favored. Pigs love overturning fresh ground and digging into promising places. Asking a pig how much space it needs is like asking a human how

Opposite: Two rows of electric wire keep Spotted Rose the sow in her place in the barnyard at The Reimanis Farm. From a pig's perspective, there's no upper limit to how large their fenced-in area should be.

much space it needs. The eyes narrow. "I don't like where this is headed. Why are you asking me that?"

In case you're thinking, "Of course they want lots of space—all animals want lots of space," think again. Consider sheep. Sheep live for fresh grass and the security of the flock. If those two needs can be met within a half-acre, that's fine with the sheep. They don't need to light out for the territories or see if the grass is greener on the other side of the fence or go west, young sheep. If the grass is green where they are, that's all they need. I've had sheep escape on our farm, and how do they look when I find them hiding behind a tree in the neighbor's yard, surrounded by green lawn? They look scared and sad.

How do pigs look when they escape? Delighted. Absolutely delighted. I don't exactly know how they convey this emotional state so succinctly, lacking full lips and eyebrows and the usual tools we humans use to communicate, but they do. Tails are up, eyes are sparkling, ears are flapping around, hooves are light. There's promise in the air.

To raise happy pigs, therefore, you really want your pig enclosure to be as big as possible. I once worked on a farm where the pig fence was strung around an area nearly an acre in size, including a section of swampy bottomland where the pigs would get lost among the alders and muck. It was great fun watching the branches heave and sway as the pigs crashed through the distant saplings on the way back to the trough at feeding time. (In hindsight, this probably wasn't so great for the swamp.)

But back in the world of limited space, how much space does a pig need? I recommend a minimum of 500 to 1,000 square feet of pen per pig. Since I'm also recommending keeping a minimum of two pigs, that means you ought to have 1,000 square feet or so to keep two pigs happy. More, of course, is better. If you have a lot of land, ten pigs per acre is the recommended stocking rate for pigs on pasture.

CLASSIC FENCING: THE PIGSTY

Where do pigs live? The simple option, of course, is the pigsty, just like Wilbur had in *Charlotte's Web*. Pigs have been housed in pigsties ever since pigs first came in from the cold to live among us humans.

In essence a pigsty is a solid wooden enclosure. The walls are typically 3 to 4 feet high—more than tall enough to contain adult pigs but also tall enough to contain scampering shoats who might want to get out, and also to deter dogs, young boys, and other wildlife that might want to get in. Sometimes sties are simply partitioned areas inside a barn or other structure; sometimes they are freestanding stockades. Throw in a roof or some other shelter for your pigs (see chapter 3), and your sty is ready to go.

The key to an effective pigsty is making it as stout as possible. Posts should be 4 by 4 inches in size (or, if you can figure out how to attach sides to them, steel T-posts work well, too) and need to be sunk at least 2 feet into the ground—3 is better. Your pigs are going to frequently rub up against these posts. Sometimes they'll be after a good scratch, sometimes they'll be bored, and sometimes they'll just want to see what will happen if they push a little harder. They are also going to root down around the posts in search of new smells and delights, easily undermining any posts that don't extend well into the earth.

Sty walls are usually solid, or nearly so, with the bottom dug into the ground 6 inches. Use 2-inch-thick wood, at least along the bottom, where pig pressure is highest. If the walls are slatted, the slats need to be firmly affixed to the posts, preferably on the inside. Your pigs are going to have all the time in the world to rub against these slats, lever them around with their prodigious snouts and necks, and discover every weak spot than can be exploited. Use screws, not nails.

You'll need a gate into the sty, and this presents a tricky proposition. Hanging a regular farm gate on steel hinges won't get the job done—that's the exact arrangement that my pigs shouldered aside in the exciting moments just before my sister's wedding reception at our farm. Your pigs will intuitively recognize that the gate is the weak link in their perimeter, and they will watch how you maneuver the latches and clasps that make it open. Your gate should be solid, firmly bolted to its hinges, and designed with the latch on the outside, where the pigs can't observe how it works. I'm serious.

Above: Pigs play in their pen at Sunrise Farm. Hog panels are a relatively inexpensive way to build a larger pen.

Here's the advantage of the traditional sty: Once it's built, it's maintenance-free. If you build a stout stockade, your worries are over. If you add an interior partition that can be swung closed to confine the pigs together in a corner, you'll be able to handle and care for them with ease. You'll also have a good setup for catching them on slaughter day.

Here's the disadvantage of the traditional sty: It's expensive and relatively arduous to build. It requires a lot of wood or other material. As a result, it tends to be too small, usually nowhere near 500 to 1,000 square feet per animal. The pigs, with very limited space in which to live and explore, end up bored, and bored pigs, like bored humans, become unpleasant pigs. You become their captor. They are no longer happy to see *you*, only the food and possibility of escape that you represent.

On top of that, your pigs will start to stink more than usual because they don't have enough space to hoof off into a remote corner to defecate in privacy. In case you were wondering why the term "pigsty" is pejorative, now you know. It's not the sty itself, it's that the sty is almost invariably too small for the pigs.

One way to increase the size of the pigsty without breaking the bank is to make use of hog panels, which are sections of welded metal fencing sold at most farm-supply stores. They typically come in 8-foot and 16-foot lengths, and in 34-inch and 48-inch heights. (I've found that the shorter height works fine for both shoats and hogs.) Hog panels aren't cheap, but they're cheaper than using solid wood and should last for many years. Drive in a post every 4 feet on the outside of the panel for adequate strength and security.

EFFICIENT FENCING: ELECTRICITY

Pigs don't seem all that impressed by most of our human inventions. A neat rubber water trough will occupy them for, at most, a few hours, until they've flipped it over a bunch of times, trampled it, and moved on. Wooden posts, steel bars, pieces of roofing—all these have a certain appeal, but after a day or two, your typical pig is already looking around for the next big thing. But there's one human invention that they don't love but definitely respect, time after time: the electric fence.

The first time I saw that farm where the pigs roamed around their acre of swampy bottomland, I thought there must have been a mistake. The only thing defining the edge of the pigs' area were two skimpy electric wires suspended from very feeble-looking flexible posts, each wire less than a foot off the ground. If you weren't paying attention, you could easily have walked right over the thing without tripping. I couldn't believe that the pigs inside that fence—smart pigs, curious pigs, pigs strong enough to flip you into the mud on your backside—did anything but laugh at such a fence.

My theory now, after watching pigs for a number of years, is that they ascribe some level of magic to an electric fence. They are smart enough to realize that the wire isn't strong enough to contain them and that they are agile enough, at least as shoats, to clear the thing easily with a running start. The only explanation I can come up with is that they are too smart; they appear to have formulated a theory of magic and, with this convenient explanation in hand, applied it to the fence. As a result, there is no easier way to contain pigs than to use electric fencing, of which there are two types.

SHEEP NETTING

The simplest way to contain pigs is to use sheep fence, which is electrified netting that comes with its own fiberglass posts built in. You simply unroll the stuff, push in the posts, and connect it to a charger. Make sure you choose a netting like ElectroNet (see appendix 2 for more information), because the vertical spacers in this type are semi-rigid plastic that help keep the fence tight and vertical between posts. Sheep netting is usually sold in rolls that are 160 feet long, so a single roll will create a nice amount of space for two pigs; two rolls will do well for four to six pigs.

Sheep netting, in truth, is taller and stouter (and, at roughly a buck a foot, more expensive) than it needs to be to contain pigs, but it's so convenient and easy to use that it may well be worth the added expense. Plus, the extra height and visibility are good for keeping unwanted intruders out of the pigpen. We live in an area with lots of coyotes, and though a hog is more than a match for a coyote, a little shoat probably isn't. Fortunately, I've never found out, because the tight weave of the sheep netting is great for deterring the canine crowd. The sheep netting is also highly visible, which prevents wandering humans from bumping into it by accident.

Three details to keep in mind if you go the sheep netting route: First is that, over the course of a long summer, the sheep netting is going to sag,

Above: Olive the dog and Maxene the pig take a look at life on the other side at Sunrise Farm. This type of electric netting fence, commonly used for sheep, is the simplest way to keep pigs in and intruders out.

especially at the corners. I recommend that you drive in a stout metal or wooden post at each corner to tighten the netting. Sink the post about a foot away from the corner, outside of the netting, and run some baling twine, strong string (or anything nonconductive) between the post and one of the netting's fiberglass posts. Tighten up on the string to put tension on the netting and keep it from sagging.

The second detail to keep in mind about netting is that it is *not* maintenance-free. Grass and weeds will grow up into the netting, shorting it out. If it gets bad enough, the weeds can get so tangled in the netting that you won't be able to roll it up again in the fall without tearing the wires and ruining the roll. About once a week, therefore, I perambulate the fence, pulling it up to untangle it from the ground and cutting back weeds and grass. I use a weed whacker, staying about 3 inches away from the netting, and then coming back and clearing right next to the fence by hand. The truly advanced technique is to clear a swath with the weed whacker and then reposition the netting posts into the center of the cleared swath. Next week, mow the swath on the other side of the fence and move the netting back to where it originally was. This cuts down on the handwork.

The third detail of netting is that you'll need a source of electricity for the fence. If you live on a farm that already has a fence charger, just run a feed line over to your pigpen and call it good. If you don't, you'll need to buy a fence charger, which will cost you some money. Buy the smallest one available—it will be more than enough to power your roll or two of sheep netting. If electricity is near at hand, buy a plug-in model, which is less expensive. If not, buy a solar-powered version with a battery, whose added price will be more than made up in added convenience if the pigpen is far from the nearest outlet. If you already own a plug-in battery charger, you can skip the solar panel; buy two batteries and swap them between the fence charger and battery charger once a week to replenish their juice.

The fence charger will come with instructions for proper installation, which includes driving at least one copper rod into the earth to ground the system. Most fence chargers work by pulsing high voltage across the fence every second or so, with the circuit being completed through the ground if an animal happens to be touching the fence. Some people mistakenly believe they can avoid installing a ground rod if the fence is small—not so! Without the ground return, the pulse is not apt to be powerful enough to deter a pig, especially one that leans in from the side, where the thick hide and bristles will provide insulation.

ELECTRIC WIRE FENCING

If you're handy with electric fencing, or just handy in general, and if the area you want to fence in for your pigs is quite large, you might consider making your own fence out of posts and electric wire. It's nowhere near as easy as unrolling the netting, but it's a less expensive option for a large pen. It's also easier to maintain in tall grass and weeds because you can mow under the bottom wire with a weed whacker and there's less wire to short out in the first place.

Start by driving in metal T-posts at the corners of your proposed pen, or anywhere that the fence will make a sharp turn. Then pound in fiberglass poles every 10 to 15 feet between the T-posts. The fiberglass posts are strong enough to suspend the wire but not strong enough to keep a corner tight, so go with the metal where needed and the less expensive fiberglass everywhere else.

There are special plastic insulators that go with each type of post, so buy enough of each to go around. You'll need two per post. Position one insulator about 6 inches off the ground, the second about 6 inches above that, with the insulators facing out, away from the center of the pen. Then run the wire around the outside of the perimeter, from insulator to insulator. Amazingly enough, these two wires will contain your pigs.

If you use metal wires, you'll need some sort of insulator at each end that you can really tug on to make the wire tight. I usually sink a wooden post at each end of the fence, nail in a beefy plastic insulator, and then pull hard to take the slack out of the wire. An even better solution is to use electric rope, which looks like plastic twine with metal woven into it—commonly sold at electric fence supply places. It doesn't kink up like metal wire and is much easier to roll and unroll. Buy a set of metal springs (designed to be used with electric fencing) and install one at each end of the rope. Then pull tight on the rope until you've compressed the springs about a third of the way—enough to keep nice tension on the fence.

Electric wires need the same weekly inspection and degrassing that netting needs. I've found that our pigs, in the course of their rootings,

will push sticks and rocks and debris up against the wires, in an almost Masada-like effort to build a ramp up and over the fence. Whether this is done entirely deliberately or not, I can't say, but the effect is the same: The pigs will be able to escape if the project goes on long enough, and it's an easier proposition for them to surmount the two wires than the netting. So as part of your weekly perambulation, kick apart any ramps in the making and toss aside any sticks or rocks that are threatening the fence.

ELECTRIC FENCE: THE GATE AND CORRAL

You're going to need to go in and out of your pigpen, which necessitates some sort of gate. The easiest of these is simply an "off" switch for the fence; turn off the fence and step over. Especially if your fence is the two-wire type, with the top wire only a foot off the ground, this is easy to do. In fact, you can leave the fence on and just step over it. The pigs will be focused on your presence inside the pen and won't be testing the fence to see if it is on or not.

The downside of this all-electric approach is that you will have no way to catch your pigs should you need to check out a limp or other ailment. You can't corner a pig up against an electric fence: Either it will squirt through the wires in fright, or you will lunge into the fence in error as the pig bulldozes past you. The first year we raised pigs, we used this all-electric approach, and it worked out fine because we never had to catch them. Our three pigs were perfectly healthy all summer long. Then we went the vodka route on slaughter day (see chapter 6), which also didn't require catching them. Nothing could have been simpler.

But the second summer, one of our piglets got off to a rough start. Unbeknownst to me at the time, he came to us with a hernia (see chapter 1 for advice on how to avoid this). On several occasions this same pig also came up lame. I would have loved to have been able to catch this piglet on a regular basis to monitor his progress, but I couldn't because of our all-electric fence. Fortunately, he outgrew his various ailments to become a healthy hog, but I decided that having a non-electric gate and corral would have been a better management decision. I recommend that you do the same.

What you want to do is build a three-sided, U-shaped, wooden corral, with a panel that can be slid across to close the fourth side. Place your feeder inside this corral so that the pigs become comfortable with it and wander in and out without fear. Then when you want to contain the pigs, fill their feeder and pull the panel closed while the pigs are eating.

This corral can either be built completely inside the electric fence, or you can build it so that the fence starts and ends on the two arms of the U. The advantages of this approach are that your friends and neighbors can lean against the wooden fence and watch the pigs eat, even leaning down to rub their ears and necks in the process. Also, you can install your gate in one side of the corral, providing you with a way of getting in and out of the pen without having to turn off the fence.

The cheapest and easiest way to build the corral is to use old wooden shipping pallets. Use good pallets that aren't cracked. Dig a trench that's as

deep as one shovel's depth and stand the pallets up in the trench, with an open end facing up. Drive metal posts down through the center holes of the open ends and 2 feet further into the ground. Then use scrap wood to nail the pallets together at the top and the bottom and to reinforce the corners. For two pigs, make your U-shaped corral with two pallets per side. For

Opposite: Gates and electric wire along the fence keep Louise and her Tamworth piglets contained at Hogwash Farm.

three or four pigs, use three pallets across the front.

THE PORTABLE PIGPEN

As discussed in chapter 3, you can use a portable pigpen that solves both your housing and your fencing needs at the same time. The portable pen contains the pigs and acts as a corral while also providing them access to fresh pasture whenever you move it. The portable pen can also be parked and surrounded by electric fencing, turning it into a standard shelter whenever that is more convenient. This past year, when the autumn rains made the ground soft and less conducive to driving the tractor around, and when the growing hogs began taking up a considerable amount of space inside the pen, I parked the pen for the final month, removed the free end, and fenced in a pasture using sheep netting. If you decide to go this route, be sure not to move the pen with the free end off, since the structure may not be sufficiently rigid to withstand the stress of movement. I also attached a 2x4 across the top of the free end to prevent the pigs from damaging the structure as they rubbed against the no-longer-supported end posts.

THE FINAL CONSIDERATION

The final consideration when it comes to fencing is deciding how your pigs' time on your farm is going to come to an end. Your answer to this question will influence the decisions you make about your fencing system.

For most people who raise pigs, the end of the line comes when the pigs are loaded onto a truck (either yours or the butcher's) for the trip to the slaughterhouse. Loading pigs onto a truck or trailer is much easier said than done. Three-hundred-pound, generally uncooperative animals—far stronger than you—need to be induced to walk up a ramp they've never seen before into a truck they don't like the looks of. Good luck.

To begin the proceedings, you don't want to be chasing the pigs across hill and dale to get them close to the truck in the first place. I tried this one afternoon with a few friends on a nearby farm. Armed with sheets of metal roofing, we played chess with the pigs, trying to box them into the corner of the pen nearest to the truck. Come evening, we were covered in mud, the slaughter appointment had been missed, and the pigs, wary, angry, and alarmed, were still at large.

To avoid the chase, you'll need some sort of corral like the one I described above. Provided you've been feeding your pigs in the corral all along, you'll at least have them contained in one spot when it comes time to load them up. A portable pigpen (see chapter 3) serves the same purpose, being a solid enclosure that permits no escape. All you need to do is figure out how to make a hefty ramp, one that is roughly 24 inches wide (wide enough for pig-passage, but not enough for pig-turning-around), strong enough to hold 500 pounds or so (you plus a 300-pound pig), and with solid sides (so that the pigs don't know they're up in the air).

I know of one farmer who backs his pickup truck up to the corral a week before slaughter day, then proceeds to feed the pigs in the truck. Come slaughter day, the pigs are already in there, ready to go. This system works because he is able to back his truck right up to (and slightly below) the pen, such that the ramp is short and close to level. The pigs can see the food from the pen—no further inducement needed.

The first year we had pigs, we had no corral and no solid enclosure of any kind. The three pigs were contained inside a pen of electric sheep netting. Very simple. On slaughter day, we soaked their grain in vodka, let them get good and soused, waited until they more or less passed out, turned off the fence, walked in, and did the deed. If this approach appeals to you, see the next chapter for more details. You may be able to avoid the whole "loading the pigs into the truck" saga altogether. The upshot for this discussion, however, is that no special corral was required.

CHAPTER SIX

Slaughter Day

A number of years ago, before I'd started raising pigs but when I was considering getting started, I met a woman at an agricultural fair who raised pigs. Then in her seventies, and after having raised pigs for most of her life, she said the only thing she didn't like about raising pigs was how terribly they squealed on slaughter day. She said it used to keep her awake at night, both before and after the event. It got so bad that at one point, she stopped raising pigs altogether.

Her words reminded me of a similar warning that another friend had given me, about how he would never raise pigs as an adult after being forced to take part in the slaughter as a child. While I stood there at the fair, reconsidering my love of pork and even my desire to start raising pigs at all, the woman turned to me and, with a spreading grin and a twinkle in her eye, blurted out, "Then I discovered vodka!"

She'd heard from someone that soaking the final morning's grain in vodka caused the pigs to fall soundly asleep, happily snoring through their final hours, oblivious both to their own fate and to the demise of the pigs sleeping right next to them. It worked, she

Opposite: Maxene, a Yorkshire cross hog, is groggy from drinking vodka mixed in with her grain. The potion works wonders in calming the pigs on slaughter day.

said. She'd started raising pigs again that year and had been raising them successfully ever since. And wasn't the meat delicious!

This was enough for me—I decided on the spot to start raising pigs myself. In my excitement, however, I forgot to ask her the key question: *How much vodka?* But I'm getting ahead of myself.

WHEN TO SLAUGHTER PIGS

Pigs are traditionally slaughtered in the fall, once summer's bounty of food has been used up and the cool weather of autumn has arrived. To a great extent, with store-bought grain available year-round and slaughterhouses having enormous coolers for chilling meat, pigs can now be raised and slaughtered in almost any month of the year. Indeed, raising pigs on something other than the typical late-spring to late-fall schedule can make it easier to schedule an appointment at a slaughterhouse and also make it easier to find shoats for sale at good prices. Provided you can keep your pigs warm through the winter, you can raise them and slaughter them anytime you like.

On our farm, with its abundance of summer vegetables and green pasture, the traditional schedule makes sense. We buy our shoats in May and usually slaughter them in mid- to late October. We also do the slaughtering ourselves, so the cool weather makes the work easier.

If you're not tied to a certain schedule, the key consideration for when to slaughter is your hogs' weight. Although pigs will continue gaining size for years and can reach a half a ton or more in weight, the efficiency at which they transform food into pork starts to diminish with time. Also, if you end up selling your hogs whole (more on this in a minute), you're going to have fewer takers for 800 pounds of pork than for 200. On the flip side, if you slaughter your hogs when they're still quite small, you're missing out on the fastest and most efficient part of the growth curve.

Most folks seem to agree that the optimal live weight for a hog ready for slaughter is about 250 pounds or so. I usually let ours grow closer to 300 pounds, given the abundance of fall apples in our neighborhood and my desire to have the vegetables put to bed before tackling the slaughter

Above: While spending part of his summer on the farm, Dan Monahan of Cambridge, MA, left, helps the author read a hog weigh tape to determine the progress of a pig. It was destined to be slaughtered soon for a pig roast at a friend's wedding.

chores. Other folks make the move when their animals pass the 200 mark. The scientific folk know exactly what the optimal weight is for their breed of hog—the moment that additional pounds start to go down in value—and slaughter on exactly the right day. I'm not that organized, but if you are, go for it.

How much does your hog weigh? Pass a measuring tape (one of those cloth tapes is best) around the belly of the hog, just behind the forelegs, and note the girth in inches. Now run the tape from the root of the tail to a line between the ears, and note that length in inches. Square the girth, multiply by the length, divide the whole thing by 400, and you'll have your hog's approximate weight in pounds. Pretty neat. You can also see if your local feed store carries a "hog weigh tape," which has the calculations built right in.

EMOTIONAL PREPARATION

Of all the emotions I expected to feel after slaughtering pigs for the first time, I was completely unprepared for the emotion I actually did feel as I headed back to the farmhouse to wash up afterward: pride.

I was tired and dirty and ready for sleep. I had clothes that badly needed to be washed. My arms were too heavy to do much beyond unzip my jacket. But I also felt a distinct skip in my step and an enormous sense of competence. It wasn't just the pride of a job well done, though I certainly felt some of that. It was the pride of tackling a job that most people find too horrifying to even consider, let alone discuss in polite company, and discovering that it wasn't so bad after all. Discovering, in fact, that it was a job full of richness and meaning, wonder and learning. An unforgettable experience. Most surprising of all, an experience to look forward to each year.

Despite this ringing endorsement, you should know—indeed, you already know—that slaughtering animals is very tricky business, emotionally more than physically. The word itself suggests much of the problem: "Slaughter" conjures terrible images in most people's minds. It's invariably used to describe brutal murders or one-sided military engagements, with special sympathy extended to the victims. Though the word "slaughter" began its life in the barnyard, its journey out into the wider world of human affairs has cast a very negative shadow back onto the farm.

Which, if you think about it for more than a moment, makes no sense at all. Killing things is an unavoidable part of being human; indeed, of being any being. It's not possible to pass through life without diverting some of nature's bounty to your own growth and development. Some may convince themselves that this bounty can be entirely of a vegetable nature, but even a brief trip into farm country demonstrates that this is a distinction without a difference. Soybeans and broccoli, two of the more-nutritious plants in the vegetable kingdom, would never make it from seed to harvest without the killing and dislocation of countless wild animals and the destruction of their habitat.

Even my most loyal farm customers, who love to eat our meat and vegetables and who "get it"—supporting our farm's holistic approach to raising meat and vegetables together—often don't want to know too much about the details of slaughtering. They love seeing the pigs on pasture one week and the meat in the freezer the next, but they don't want to know about the gun and the box of knives and the bucket full of guts.

This widespread antipathy toward slaughtering has led to the natural result that almost nobody wants to slaughter animals anymore and even fewer people know how to do it well. Raising animals specifically for food is a foundation block of civilization, a practice dating back tens of thousands of years, but you're going to be lucky to find even a handful of people who know anything about it. This is, at a minimum, going to present a logistical problem for you, the pig raiser, regardless of whether you want to slaughter your pigs yourself or find someone else to do the job for you.

Even so, your own emotional preparation is the hardest part of the process. If you were to walk around the corner of a building one afternoon and come across a couple of people in the middle of slaughtering a pig, you'd very likely be shocked and upset. I would be, too. I'm convinced that every human with a heart and the ability to feel compassion would be upset. Imagine how awful it would be *not* to feel upset at the unexpected sight of a dead animal?

In the days leading up to a scheduled slaughter on our farm, I find myself thinking about the slaughter frequently. It's often on my mind first thing in the morning, especially on the appointed day. I picture what a dead pig looks like. I visualize holding the knife and making the important incisions. I see blood on my hands and make a note to roll up my sleeves beforehand. I run through the logistical steps in my mind, making sure that we have the tools and equipment we'll need and enough people to do the job right.

Although it used to bother me that I couldn't stop thinking about the slaughter in the days leading up to it—I saw it as a sign of weakness somehow—I've now come to realize that this visualization is an essential part of the emotional preparation. You don't want to be surprised on slaughter day. You don't want to be the person walking around the building, caught unawares. You don't want to catch a glimpse through the slaughterhouse door and suddenly feel queasy. You want to have a sense of how things are going to go so that you can remain calm and relaxed through the process.

You owe that to the pigs, just as much as to yourself. Pigs are extraordinarily perceptive, not just of their physical surroundings but also of your moods and intentions. Pigs are said to be smarter than dogs, in whatever way that is measured, and dogs are renowned for their ability to sense when a regular old trip in the car is about to turn into a trip to the vet's office. Think about your pigs—you don't want to needlessly stress them by being unduly stressed yourself. Whatever your thoughts are about slaughter day, work them out in advance.

OPTION ONE: THE SLAUGHTERHOUSE

In some ways, the easiest way to transition your pigs from living creatures into paper-wrapped cuts of meat is to take the pigs to a slaughterhouse. The staff are, presumably, trained professionals who know their work and know how to conduct animal slaughter in a way that both respects the sanctity of the animal's life and maximizes the quality and quantity of the resulting meat. Many people think that slaughtering animals is barbarous and primitive work; in fact, it should be neither.

Take a tour of the slaughterhouse before you commit to bringing your pigs in. The facilities should be clean and well lit, not just on the meat-processing side (where dirt and debris can lead to contamination of the meat) but also in the animal waiting area. You're not going to be on hand when your pigs are killed, so you can only infer how the process is going to go from their perspective. If you see that the holding pens are caked with manure and that the waiting animals are clearly stressed and unhappy, you can be sure that conditions are not going to improve for them as they move onto the killing floor. Take your business elsewhere.

There is, however, one major logistical problem involved with taking your pigs to a slaughterhouse, and that is getting the pigs into the truck or trailer at the outset. This is a detail that appears minor and easily addressed from the safety of several months away but starts to loom increasingly large as the day approaches. Indeed, without some forethought, it can be all but insurmountable. Lambs can be picked up and hefted into a truck if needed. Chickens can be loaded six at a time. Not pigs. Pigs need to walk in under their own power.

Pigs, particularly hogs weighing in the neighborhood of 300 pounds, and especially hogs that have grown suspicious of your intentions toward them for the day, can resemble inanimate boulders. Levers and chocks seem like the only helpful tools for prying them up a ramp and into a waiting truck. That is, until your pig catches a glimpse of freedom, at which point the boulder will suddenly move with all the force and inevitability of a steep-mountain landslide. Heading, invariably, away from the truck.

With luck, you've already read the chapter in this book on fencing and have built an appropriate corral or loading area. To recap, this area needs to be made from stout posts, clad with thick wooden or metal paneling that extends down into the ground at least six inches, and that has a pig-proof gate. Ideally, your pigs will be tightly crowded into this area so that the inevitable pig landslide doesn't have the chance to pick up any speed. You're also going to need a loading ramp made from 2-inch-thick (minimum) lumber to support the pigs (and your) weight that has solid sides so that the pigs won't see themselves leaving the ground.

Here are a few more details that can make the loading go easier. If your pigpen is on a sloping piece of land, back the trailer up below the pen so that the ramp is less steep between pen and trailer. If the pen is indoors, use the building's loading dock so that you don't need a ramp at all. If you have time to wait, move the pig's feeder into the trailer and feed the final morning's rations there. With luck, the pigs' hunger will overcome their wariness, and they'll walk up the ramp in due time.

One approach I've heard about is of a woman who feeds her pigs every day by backing up her pickup truck to the pen and tossing the food directly from the truck into the pig's feeder. The pigs, as you can imagine, quickly develop a fondness for the truck. On occasions when the pigs escape their pen, she drives out in the truck, and the pigs follow it right back to the pen. On slaughter day, all she has to do is set up the ramp and avoid being trampled as the pigs hustle their way into the truck. The pigs, happy and enthusiastic and not stressed in the least, end up doing all the work.

OPTION TWO: HIRE SOMEONE TO COME TO YOUR PLACE

A second option is to have a professional come to your place to do the slaughtering. The three great benefits here are that there's no loading to be done, the pigs aren't stressed by being moved to an unfamiliar location, and you can keep an eye on things. This last point, of course, is also the potential downside: you'll need to keep an eye on things. But if you're willing and able, there's nothing better for the pigs than being able to live out their final moments at home.

What usually happens is that the slaughterer (or slaughtering crew) will come to your place, do the deed, and then bring the carcasses back to their butcher shop for hanging, cutting, and wrapping. Confer with them in advance to see what equipment they will bring and what you will need to provide. The key items are a tripod and winch for lifting the pig carcass up off the ground (this could be a tractor with a bucket, if you have one in the neighborhood), a sawhorse or similar platform for working on the pig, and barrels or tubs for collecting the guts.

Most slaughterers will take the guts and debris with them, often for an added disposal fee. Work this detail out beforehand. If you decide to dispose of the guts on your own property, you'll want to bury everything where marauding dogs and other animals can't get at it. For a 300-pound

Opposite: Mark Durkee of Chelsea, VT, skins a pig on a customer's farm in Tunbridge, VT. Slaughtering animals on site, Durkee does the work his father and grandfather did before him.

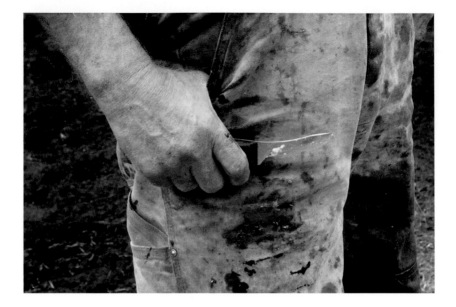

pig, you're talking 80 pounds or so of guts, feet, hide, and head—not a trivial amount. In Vermont, the requirement is that the guts be buried at least 2 feet underground and at least 100 feet from the nearest water source. Check with your local agricultural extension office to make sure you're in compliance with all the appropriate regulations before you head out with the shovel.

Another detail to discuss with the slaughterer is whether to skin or scald your pigs. Skinning is the easier approach, but for those who like pork rinds, or the flavor that comes with keeping the skin on the shoulder roast, scalding is the way to go. For scalding, the whole pig is immersed in a tub of boiling water to loosen the bristles, which are then scrubbed off with a brush. If you can't quite picture how to maneuver a 300-pound hog into and out of a vat of boiling water without grievously injuring yourself or the meat, you'll see why many people go the skinning route. But if your slaughterer knows the drill and has the equipment, this is an option to consider.

As for how the slaughterer will go about the job and what your role will be during all this, and whether you want to have some vodka on hand, the complete picture is painted in the next section.

OPTION THREE: DO IT YOURSELF

Here's where the vodka comes in. After a few years of trial and error, in which the error mostly was me mixing too little vodka into the grain, I've settled on a quart of vodka per pig. This is about right, assuming your pigs weigh between 250 and 300 pounds or so. You could probably go up to a quart and a half if you really wanted to knock them out, but don't go much beyond that. You don't, ironically enough, want to kill them.

The strategy is not to feed your pigs at all the night before. Then, in the morning, pour the appropriate amount of vodka into a bucket. Add just enough grain to soak up all the liquid (this usually takes fifteen minutes or so). Then drizzle on some honey or molasses to mask the pungency of the alcohol. Finally, feed the whole mash to the pigs, who should gobble it up hungrily. Throw in some crushed apples or any other sweet treat if the pigs seem to be balking at the alcohol.

While they are eating, arrange their fencing so that they can't crawl off into some distant corner and fall asleep where you can't get to them. Close a gate around their feeding area or corral, or put up some electric netting to contain them. Once they finish eating, give them an hour or two for the vodka to take full effect. At this point, you'll have about four to five hours before they start to sober up. They may not actually fall asleep on you, but the vodka dulls their senses and makes them less cognizant of what's going on around them.

The first year that I slaughtered pigs, a knowledgeable friend came to help me. We needed about two hours to kill, skin, and gut each animal, so we were just able to start the third pig before it sobered up. More recently, I've had two friends help, and we have been able to process each pig in about an hour, meaning that we can now comfortably slaughter four pigs

before the vodka starts to lose its hold on the final one. If it's your first time out, I recommend giving yourself plenty of time so that you don't feel rushed—try having at least one person per pig on hand to help.

LEGAL RAMIFICATIONS

Before getting into the nitty-gritty of slaughtering, there's a legal consideration to keep in mind. If your ultimate intention is to sell your pork by the individual piece—a package of chops, say, or a whole ham—you'll need to have the animals slaughtered under either USDA inspection or the regulations that apply in your home state. This means that you'll have

Above: Yorkshire cross hogs Patty, foreground, and LaVerne doze after eating a mixture of vodka and grain on slaughtering day at Sunrise Farm.

to take the pigs to an officially registered slaughterhouse. The inspector, naturally enough, wants to see that each pig is alive and healthy prior to slaughter, so slaughtering the pigs at home and bringing in the carcasses isn't an option.

The alternative is to sell your pigs whole, not in pieces. If someone knows you well enough to arrange to buy a whole animal from you, the government figures, "caveat emptor." The government's goal is to prevent anonymous meat from contaminating the food supply, and buying a whole pig from your neighbor is anything but anonymous.

Under this whole-hog approach, you sell the animal based on its "hanging weight," which is the weight of the carcass after it's been slaughtered (head, feet, guts, and hide removed) but before it's been butchered (sliced into individual cuts of meat). Once the carcass has been butchered, the individual packages of meat are stamped NOT FOR SALE to indicate that they are not allowed to make their way into the retail food world. Your customers, meanwhile, agree that the meat is only for themselves, their immediate family, and their non-paying guests.

While I believe that the government has a role to play in protecting food safety, I can't help but notice that this particular regulation puts backyarders like you and me at a distinct disadvantage in the marketplace. While many people like pork, very few have the wherewithal (or freezer space) to buy an entire pig at one time. Even pricing the meat below retail, which I do, can't entirely overcome the difficulty in finding customers. By all rights, your pork should be priced far above retail levels, given how much better it is than the bland stuff that usually lurks in the butcher case.

I hope the USDA will one day provide an exemption for us backyarders so that we can sell a certain amount of pork, in individual cuts, directly from farm to consumer. Meanwhile, the current arrangement does have an upside: You end up selling every cut of meat equally. If you were selling retail packages out of a freezer, for example, the bacon and pork chops would sell out immediately. All you'd have for yourself would be ham ends, a shoulder roast or two, and some miscellaneous sausage.

SLAUGHTER TOOLS AND EQUIPMENT

If you've decided to go the official USDA/slaughterhouse route, you don't need to read on. But if you're thinking of either doing the slaughter your-self or hiring someone to come and do it at your place, read on. Here's the list of tools and equipment you'll need:

Vodka and grain

Hose, water, and scrub brushes

One 8-inch kitchen knife

One 3-inch skinning or paring knife for each person

One small, sharp hatchet or ax

Tractor with bucket (or some other system, like a winch and tripod)
    for raising the carcass off the ground

Length of chain with cinch ring on one end

Handgun or rifle

One gambrel or set of hooks for each pig

3- to 4-foot, sturdy, v-shaped sawhorse

Reciprocating saw or butcher's handsaw

Place for one carcass to cool while the tractor or tripod is being
    used for another

Box of contractor-grade trash bags

Barrels or trash cans for collecting guts

STEP ONE: THE SHOT

With the pigs drunk and your crew assembled, step one is shooting the first animal. Your goal is to send a bullet right through the top of the skull and into the brain, killing the animal instantly. Picture an imaginary x that joins the right eye to the left ear and the left eye to the right ear. Then aim just slightly to the side of where the two lines cross and pull the trigger. (I actually aim right into the

 Above: Carl Demrow of Washington, VT, uses a large-caliber handgun to take aim at a pig to be slaughtered at Sunrise Farm.

middle of the x, assuming that the bullet will go in slightly off-center in the uncertainty of the moment.)

If your pig is asleep or standing still, aiming like this is easy. If not, and your pig is staggering around, place some grain or other favored food on the ground right in front of it. When the pig bends to eat, you'll have a steady target. You want the head to be down when you shoot so that the bullet, if it passes through the skull, ends up in the ground under the pig, not lodged farther back in the carcass.

We use a large-caliber handgun to do the shooting because the handgun is easy to hold and the large, slow-moving bullet inflicts maximal damage. I'm not interested in cutting it close at this point and risking wounding the animal—I want to make sure that there's no question about the lethality of the shot. Professional slaughterers, however, typically use a .22 caliber rifle, the inexpensive, lightweight gun most often used for target shooting. If you are confident in your marksmanship and your nerves, be my guest. I'm sticking with the handgun.

STEP TWO: BLEEDING OUT

As soon as the pig is shot, it will collapse on the ground and start to twitch. This is always the hardest moment for me to witness because, even though the animal is dead, it is moving spasmodically as the nervous system fires irregularly in death. (If only the body collapsed like a sack of potatoes, like they so often do in the movies!) Despite this distraction, your job is to approach the pig as quickly as possible and slit the animal's throat, making sure to completely sever one of the carotid arteries that runs up each side of the neck. A sharp, 8-inch kitchen knife is ideal for this task. Stab the knife straight into the middle of the side of the neck, just behind the ear, and cut downward, toward the throat. The spurt of blood from the severed artery will indicate that you've done the job right.

Doing this quickly is important because the animal's twitching muscles will pump the blood out of the carcass, ensuring the

Opposite: Kevin Comeau of White River Junction, VT, cleans a freshly slaughtered pig at Sunrise Farm. Cleaning the carcass thoroughly while the hide is still on makes for clean meat later on.

highest-quality meat. Drag the carcass so that the opened neck is downhill from the rest of the body, allowing gravity to assist with the bleeding. Better yet, loop a chain around one of the rear legs and use a tractor bucket to lift the carcass up off the ground. The heavy bleeding will be over in a few minutes.

STEP THREE: CLEANING THE HIDE

Because a pig's hide is usually covered in dust and mud, and because you don't want your meat to be covered in either of these, take this opportunity to thoroughly clean off the hide. At our farm, we hang the carcass from the tractor bucket, which allows us to drive the carcass out of the pen (away from the remaining pigs) and also start the cleaning process while the bleeding is still under way. If you don't have a tractor, use a truck or a bunch of people to drag the carcass out of the pen and a tripod and winch to raise the entire carcass up off the ground.

Using a hose and a brush, scrub the pig's hide from tail to snout, loosening all dirt and mud as you go. It's tempting to cut corners here and just partially rinse the hide off, but time spent now will more than make up for time saved later trying to clean specks of dirt and debris off of the meat. If you're planning to take the carcasses to a butcher shop for cutting and wrapping, in fact, you won't be allowed in the door if the meat has any sign of contamination. So spend five or ten minutes now to thoroughly clean the hide.

STEP FOUR: REMOVING THE FEET AND HEAD

With the carcass clean, maneuver the tractor (or maneuver the sawhorse under the tripod) so that you can lie the carcass down, on its back, on top of the sawhorse. Not just any old sawhorse will do here—you need a very sturdy unit, 3 feet long, with sides that are about a foot high on either side to prevent the carcass from rolling

Opposite: Norah Lake of Grafton, VT, and Demrow use a sawhorse to begin the skinning process. The sawhorse holds the carcass at a convenient height while keeping it clean.

Above: Lake uses a razor blade for the
fine work at Sunrise Farm.

off. The pig should lie snugly in the v of the sawhorse, with the head and tail protruding from either end and the belly facing up.

The next step is to cut off the four feet, which often still have some mud on them despite your best cleaning efforts. If you're handy with the knife, you can remove the four feet by cutting through the wrist joints. Apply sideways pressure to the bones of the joint by levering the foot perpendicular to its normal direction of movement. This will place the wrist tendons under tension and cause them to snap as you cut into them with the knife. Continue cutting all the way through the joint as it opens up.

If you're not as handy with a knife, or if the preceding paragraph doesn't make any sense to you, another approach is to use a reciprocating saw (or even a handsaw) to cut through the bone to remove the feet. Sterilize the saw blade with bleach before you get started. If you use a reciprocating saw, use the coarse-toothed wood blade, not the fine-toothed metal blade, which will quickly clog and dull. To keep things simple, I prefer to cut through the bone just below the joint rather than through the joint itself, where all the moving parts are apt to splinter.

Whether cutting or sawing, you want to make sure not to cut the Achilles tendons that run up the back of the rear legs. Before we're done with the slaughtering, we're going to resuspend the carcass by its hind legs, and the easiest way to do that is by passing a hook behind the Achilles tendon. On the rear legs, the wrist joint is only an inch or so above the hoof (and just below the dewclaws)—don't cut through the more obvious elbow joint by mistake. The joints on the front legs are 4 to 6 inches above the hooves and easier to locate.

To remove the head, pull open the cut you previously made in the neck during bleeding and deepen it until you can see the spinal column. Locate a disk of cartilage between two vertebrae and cut through the column. Once you're through, continue cutting through the flesh on the opposite side of the neck until the head is completely free. If your taste runs to tongue or jowls, save the head for later processing. If not, discard it in the bucket with the feet.

STEP FIVE: OPENING THE HIDE

With the feet and head off, the way is now clear to start removing the hide. Using either a skinning knife or a very sharp 2- to 3-inch paring knife, slice the hide down the inside of the four legs. Start at the end of the legs, where you can see how thick the hide is from where you cut the feet off, and work your way down toward the belly. Pull back the hide with one hand as you slice under the skin with the other. Your goal is to remove the hide without cutting into the meat underneath and without removing too much of the fat. Pulling the hide back with one hand is the key to doing this, since it creates tension that allows you to see where hide and fat come together. Make shallow cuts with the knife right at this intersection. Don't switch hands as you go—keep one hand on the hide (the dirtier hand) and the other, cleaner one on the knife.

Work your way down the inside of each leg until the rear cuts come together and the front cuts come together. Then work your way along the centerline of the belly to join front to rear. Be especially careful along the belly to preserve as much fat as possible—since this is where the bacon comes from—and not to puncture the muscular wall, since you don't want to rupture the guts.

You now have opened a giant x in the hide along the belly of the carcass. Continue to peel back the hide from this x until you reach the

Above: Working in the shade helps keep the meat cool.

sawhorse sides and run out of room. When you reach the tail, cut it off roughly flush and continue easing the hide back. At the anus, leave about a ¼-inch ring of hide all the way around the hole and continue working the hide back.

STEP SIX: REMOVING THE HIDE

At this point, with the hide pulled back all the way to the sawhorses and the head, feet, and tail removed, rehang the carcass from its hind legs. A butcher's gambrel is useful here—a metal rod with sharp spikes on each end—as can be a pair of pulp hooks. Pass the hooks behind the Achilles tendons and lift the carcass up off the sawhorse, being sure that the carcass does not fall on the ground in the process. Cleanliness is crucial.

Once the carcass is suspended, the hide can be removed from the back. Some hides are loose enough that two or three people can use their combined weight to simply pull it off. Cutting a few slits in the loose hide to serve as handholds makes it easier to get a grip on the slippery hide. (If you have plans to use the intact hide, however, just roll up a few inches of hide and grab that.) If the hide is tight, or gets stuck here and there, use the paring knife to loosen the stuck spot and then pull again. Eventually, you'll pull the hide all the way down the back and off of the carcass. Sometimes this process goes smoothly, and you'll feel like a pro. Other times you have to work for every inch and feel as though time is getting away.

STEP SEVEN: GUTTING THE CARCASS

No amount of descriptive writing on my part (or perhaps nothing less than a whole chapter) can adequately describe the anatomical ins and outs of evisceration without leaving you confused, so if you don't have a seasoned hand helping you by now, grab one! It's not that the process is overly difficult; it's just that there are too many sights to be seen and taken in without the help of a guide.

Nevertheless, here goes. Start by making a careful incision about 2 inches long through the muscles of the abdominal wall, along the center-line, and roughly midway between the rib cage and where the belly button would be if pigs had belly buttons. Use your paring knife and slice very gently with little pressure, allowing the muscle and fascia to pull back from the incision. After a ½-inch or so, your knife will finish cutting through the flesh and reveal the inside of the abdominal cavity.

Put two fingers in through the slit and pull the abdominal wall out toward you, creating some space between the muscles and the viscera within. Use your fingers as a guide on either side of the centerline to pro-

Above: The author starts the gutting process by determining where to make a cut in the abdominal wall.

tect the viscera as you now extend the incision all the way from the rib cage to the pelvis. Your goal is to completely open the abdominal cavity without so much as nicking the viscera, the contents of which will contaminate the meat.

If your carcass is that of a male pig, cut just to one side of the penis, being careful not to cut the urethra that runs from the penis back to the pelvis. Once the main incision is completed, cut along the other side of the penis and urethra to remove them from the muscle wall all the way back to the pelvis. Then cut through the urethra, being careful to hold the penis away from the carcass in case there is urine in the tube.

Now return to the end of your incision at the rib cage and extend it across the sternum all the way up the neck. You needn't be quite as careful with the knife here because the sternum is protecting the organs within, and because these organs—lungs and heart—will not contaminate the meat if punctured. Use your paring knife to completely remove the breastbone by cutting through the cartilage buttons along both sides that connect it to the ribs.

At this point, you will have completely opened the carcass, and the viscera will be ready to spill out. Place the gut pail under the carcass, if you haven't done so already, and start pulling the guts out of the carcass. There will be two places where the viscera are firmly attached to the carcass and require cutting. The first of these is the diaphragm, the muscle that separates the heart and lungs from the liver and intestines. Use your knife to cut the diaphragm away from the inside of the rib cage, being careful not to cut any organs and erring on the side of the rib cage, which won't be harmed by a knife nick or two.

The second place that will require cutting is the pelvis, where the rectum and urethra pass through. The tail-end of the pelvis is a donut-shaped ring, with the rectum and urethra passing through the center. Using a very sharp hatchet or strong knife, chip away at the front of this ring, right where the two legs come together below the anus. The bone is about a

Above: Once the carcass has been cut in half, Demrow, left, and the author load the sides onto a pickup truck bed to continue cooling.

½-inch thick here, so some good pressure will be required, though there is some cartilage here that will yield easily on a young pig. When it is severed, the tension on the legs from the gambrel will pull the break open. Pull back on each leg to further open the cut and gain access to the inside of the ring.

Now use your paring knife to cut around the anus, separating it from the fascia around the pelvis, and pull it forward and out. This is often easier said than done, especially if the cracked pelvis doesn't swing open wide enough for you to see what you're doing. Go slowly, take your time, and use

Above: Slaughtering's alternative: In a moment out of *Charlotte's Web*, Clearwater the hog was saved from a trip to the butcher by Vicky Parra Tebbetts at Maple Grove Farm in Cabot, VT. Tebbetts was later married on her husband's family farm. Featured on several Christmas cards, Clearwater is now eight years old and weighs 600 pounds.

114 Living with Pigs

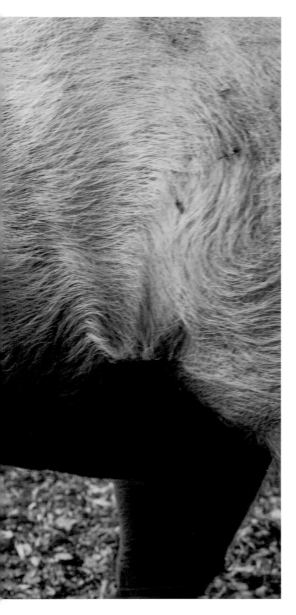

gentle pressure so as not to rupture the colon as you slowly remove it. The carcass should now be clean and gutted. If you want to save the heart, liver, or kidneys (or intestines, for sausage casings), set them aside.

Step Eight: Separating the Sides

The final step in pig slaughtering is separating the carcass into two sides. Here is where the reciprocating saw is especially useful, since it will accomplish in a minute or two what would take ten minutes or more with a handsaw. Stand on the belly side of the carcass so that you can see the spinal column and muscles on either side (the two muscles on either side of the spinal column inside the legs are the tenderloins—you don't want to nick these!) and simply cut the carcass in half, right down the middle. Make sure that each rear leg is firmly attached to the gambrel or hooks before finishing the cut, as the sides will swing free.

With the sides now separated, allow them to cool in the air and in the shade. In a slaughterhouse, the sides would now be hung in a 35-degree cooler to speed things up, so do what you can to mimic that process. We slaughter our pigs in late October in Vermont, where the temperature is usually very obliging.

BUTCHERING THE CARCASS

Here is where I have to leave you. I hope to someday have the skills and equipment to butcher our pigs, but that day has not yet come. Once the carcasses have cooled, I pull a contractor-grade trash bag (usually three mils thick and more than tall enough) around the side of pork, maneuver it into the back of the pickup truck, and tape the bag firmly closed. (Use a second bag from the opposite direction if the first isn't tall enough.) If you have a van or closed truck, that would be even better, since the goal here is to keep the sides absolutely clean and pristine on the way to the butcher's. Our local butcher is a USDA-approved facility, and even though my pigs aren't being officially inspected, they could close down his whole operation if they introduced dirt and contamination into the facility.

SLAUGHTERING FOR A PIG ROAST

This past year, one of our pigs became the centerpiece for a friend's wedding. I discovered that there are a few variations to take into account when preparing a pig for a pig roast.

The first is size. You want about a pound of roasted pig (hanging weight) per person, which means, for example, that an animal weighing 130 pounds live will be about right for 100 guests. The second detail is that the hide stays on the pig, though the bristles should be removed. Scalding and scraping is an option here, though in our case, not having a scalding vat, we used a dog clipper to shave off the bristles. Simple—took about ten minutes. I suppose a straight blade would work, too, if you knew how to use one.

The third detail is not to split the pelvis open during gutting, since the intact pelvic girdle holds the pig on the spit. Instead, take two pieces of string and tie off the ends of the rectum so that you can pull it down through the pelvis without dirtying the meat. Finally, detail four is to place a block of wood in the pig's mouth to hold it open while the carcass cools. One end of the roasting spit passes through the mouth, and if rigor mortis has set in with the jaw closed, it can be difficult for the roaster to open it back up again.

And now you know why a roasted pig always has an apple in its mouth. It's much more attractive than a gaping maw.

CHAPTER SEVEN

Pork Details

A well-cooked cheek of bacon, with roast chicken, is a dish for an epicure.

—JOSEPH HARRIS

I confess that I wasn't 100 percent sold on raising pigs until I put the first bite of pork chop into my mouth. Sure, I'd enjoyed having pigs around that first summer and had been amazed at how funny they were and how fast they grew. But they also required a certain amount of work—mental attention, really, more than physical labor—at a time of year when our retail vegetables, lambs, and chickens were already vying for my time and energy. I had enjoyed the pigs, but hadn't been fully smitten.

Then the meat came home from the butcher. I took a package of pork chops (fresh, never frozen), seared them quickly on a cast-iron skillet, added onions, apple slices, salt, pepper, and a little white wine, cooked the liquid down for ten minutes or so, slid the chops onto my plate, picked up fork and knife, and . . .

Opposite: Dotted Rose, a sow cross of Gloucestershire Old Spots, Landrace, and Tamworth, casts a wary eye upon a visitor to The Reimanis Farm. The family has been raising pigs on the farm for the past ten years.

Wow. Really. It was like having a pork chop for the first time. It was like when *The Wizard of Oz* goes from black-and-white into Technicolor. It was the heat, the freshness, the flavor, the aroma. Most of all, it was the satisfaction of

knowing that these pigs had led wonderful lives on our farm and that this meat was as good as meat ever gets.

The calls started coming in immediately from the friends to whom I had sold the other pigs. "Chuck—have you tasted the chops yet? Wow!" "Chuck—I just cooked the first ham—unbelievable." "Chuck—I know I told you I loved the chops, but would it be possible to grow a pig that was all bacon?" One of my friends was so enthusiastic that he insisted on inviting me over to try some of the pork, knowing full well that I had a freezer full of the very same stuff. He just couldn't believe that I knew what he was

Above: A newborn piglet greets her mother, Little Honey, at the The Reimanis Farm. "We like to provide our community with a good source of local, fresh, well-raised meat," said Kate Reimanis.

talking about until he witnessed me eating it with him.

My favorite testimonial of all, however, came from a close friend of mine who had been a strict vegetarian for thirty-plus years. Over at another friend's house, after listening to the gasps and exclamations and exaltations, she was induced to try a slice of ham. Skeptically at first, but then with gathering speed, she finished the slice and asked for a second.

"But aren't you a vegetarian?" I inquired later.

"As far as I'm concerned," she replied, "that wasn't meat."

I'm not telling you this to brag about my ability to raise pigs. I'm merely relaying the divine pleasure that comes from eating pigs that you've raised yourself—happy pigs, satisfied pigs, contented pigs. The emotions come straight from the pigs to the meat to you.

Which brings us to the details of the various cuts of meat. If your experience eating pork hasn't extended much beyond bacon and ham and pork chops—which mine hadn't until I started living with pigs myself—here are some of the key details to keep in mind, both for the butcher and your customers.

THE FINE PRINT

As discussed in the previous chapter, your legal choices when it comes to the pork are to eat all the meat yourself, sell each animal whole, or have the slaughter done under inspection so that you can sell the meat retail and in individual packages. If you've chosen the latter route, you're all set at this point—no further paperwork is required. If you've elected to sell the animals whole or keep the meat yourself, your butcher will likely require you to sign a waiver stating that you will not be selling the meat retail. Don't be surprised—this is standard practice.

INSTRUCTING THE BUTCHER—CUTS OF MEAT

At this point, the butcher will ask you how you want the carcass to be prepared. There are lots of options here, but I'll review the basics so that you have a starting place. If you are a gourmet chef of sorts, or are selling a hog to a friend who is serious about food, you probably know all this and more already. But if not, this review will get you in the door and keep you from embarrassing yourself in front of the butcher.

HAM

There's a whole world of choice in ham alone, but in the general sense, ham refers to the meat from the hog's hind legs.

- **Fresh ham**. By convention, ham is almost always cured, though it is certainly possible to have your butcher prepare "fresh ham," which is to say, uncured ham. Either with the bone in or out, fresh ham roasts are among the leanest meat on the animal and, cooked in liquid to prevent drying out, are wonderful.

- **Salted ham**. Salting is the most common way of curing ham, often in combination with subsequent smoking. Ham that is exclusively cured in salt can be very salty indeed—make sure you soak and rinse the meat several times to remove the excess salt before cooking.

- **Smoked ham**. Ham that is lightly salted, spiced, and smoked is what most people think of when they think "ham." The curing gives the ham a wonderfully complex flavor and also cooks it, meaning that all you need to do as the chef is heat it back up (or have it sliced thinly for sandwiches).

- **Sugar-cured (or honey-cured) ham.** When lots of sugar (or honey) is used in the curing process, the result is a sweet ham.

- **Dry-cured ham.** Prosciutto is the most famous of the dry-cured hams, which typically take six months to a year to properly age. Your butcher is unlikely to dry-cure your ham for you, so if you want to go this route, you're probably on your own.

- **Picnic ham.** Actually, this isn't ham at all; it's from the hog's front leg, not the back leg, but since it's cured the way ham is, the name has rubbed off (along with the salt and smoke).

- **Canned ham.** Actually, this isn't ham either; it's ham parts ground together and stuffed into a can. I don't include this as one of your options for the butcher, but rather to remind you of how lucky you are to be enjoying real ham from real pigs!

In all likelihood, your butcher is only going to offer one type of curing for your ham, but you still have the choice of how the ham should be cut up. A whole ham can weigh 20 pounds or more—far too much to be eaten by two people in a reasonable length of time. (Indeed, the folk definition of "eternity" is two people sitting down with a whole ham.) But for a festive occasion or holiday meal, a whole ham, slowly cooked with cloves and a sugar glaze, is a showstopper. Leftovers can easily be cubed and frozen for later snacking.

Alternatively, you can have the ham cut in half by the butcher, into the butt end and the shank end. A variation on this is to keep one half intact (say the shank) and have the other half sliced into center-cut ham steaks. This is my personal preference, since it provides the maximum variety. Then I leave the other ham (the hog has two legs) entirely whole so as to have cause to hold a big gathering on a winter's evening.

BACON

Second only to ham in popularity (or maybe not—maybe it's *more* popular!) is bacon, which is the smoked meat from the hog's belly. As I mentioned at

Above: A hog burrows into the snow to investigate at Luna Bleu Farm. The farm raises two litters per year for organic meat.

the start of the chapter, I've had more than one customer inquire about whether the entire animal could be turned into bacon, dispensing with the other cuts. (The answer—unfortunately, I guess— is no.) As with ham, you'll need to involve a smokehouse in making your bacon unless your butcher provides both services. Options to consider are thinly sliced bacon, which makes crispy strips, or thickly sliced (also known as country-style), which retains more hamlike flavor even when crisped.

In colonial times, when smoking pork seems to have been much less common than salting it, pork bellies were salted and stored in casks as "salt pork." If those sailors and homesteaders only knew how close they were to having bacon!

CANADIAN BACON

Related to bacon only in that it also comes from a pig, true Canadian bacon is made from the loin, not the belly, and is pickled, not smoked. If your butcher has pickling facilities, you're in luck. If not, you'll either have to pickle it yourself or else settle for what most people think of as Canadian bacon (people who eat in the fast-food world, that is): smoked ham cut into round circles.

CHOPS

Number three on the list of popular cuts of pork are the venerable pork chops. These practically qualify as fast food—fifteen minutes in a skillet and you're done. Options for the butcher are for single thickness, double thickness, or double thickness suitable for stuffing (with a slice nearly all the way through the middle). If you plan to cook your chops in a skillet, the single-thickness chops are quicker and easier. If baking in the oven is your plan, try the double-thickness chops. Either way, make sure to cook your chops with some sort of liquid to keep them from becoming dry and tough. Pork chops are cut from the relatively lean tenderloin, without much fat for keeping things tender.

TENDERLOIN

As you may have just deduced, you can't butcher for both chops and tenderloin because the tenderloin is the muscle that runs alongside the vertebrae. If you have your heart set on a scrumptious pork tenderloin, therefore, make sure to instruct the butcher to package it intact for roasting or grilling.

RIBS

Ribs are another favorite cut of pork (all right, are there any nonfavorite cuts of pork?). You should decide in advance how much you like ribs, since

they are cut from the side of the hog between the belly (the bacon) and the spine (chops.) If you love ribs, you can have the butcher steal some of the meat and fat from the adjacent cuts to create really meaty ribs. If bacon and chops are your preference, you'll still end up with some great ribs, just not quite as over-the-top.

SHOULDER

Your options with the shoulder are to create roasts (bone in or deboned), or have everything ground up for sausage or cut up for stir-frying or stews. My lamb customers prefer stew meat to roasts; my pork customers prefer

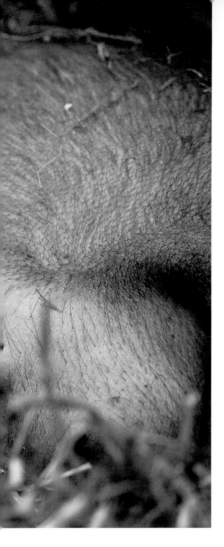

 Above: Farmer Nancy LaRowe encourages a newborn piglet to nurse from its mother's teats at Hogwash Farm. With eighteen sows on the farm, LaRowe has thirty-six litters a year to manage.

roasts to sausage. (You'll still end up with some sausage either way—just not as much if you keep the roasts whole.)

SAUSAGE

Finally, there is sausage, which is what the butcher will do with all the scraps that are too small to be packaged as individual cuts. Many butchers will offer you either breakfast sausage, which is usually either mildly spiced or not spiced at all, or some sort of hot sausage, according to their preferred recipe. This probably won't be sausage links; it will be ground sausage suitable for browning in a skillet or adding to a stew or other dish.

Beyond these "usual" cuts of pork, there is everything else, some of which may be of interest. You can request that the butcher set aside and package the various organ meats, including the heart, kidneys, and liver. (If brains are what you're after, you'll probably have to do the slaughtering yourself, since a fair bit of effort is required to extract them from the skull.) Other potentially delectable cuts include the tongue, the trotters (the feet), the jowls (which, if good and meaty, can be smoked for bacon), and the shanks (the leg ends closest to the feet, which are great when simmered in a stew).

You'll have to work out the various details with your butcher, but this should give you a general idea of what to expect. Your butcher may or may not also do the smoking and may or may not be willing to venture far into the world of organ meats and custom cutting. Good luck.

FOOD SAFETY—COOKING PORK

Who among us doesn't have some lingering sense of *pork isn't safe to eat* in the back of our minds? Who hasn't seen a delectable slice of pink, juicy pork and inadvertently thought, "Too pink? Trichinosis?"

The good news is that, if you've raised your pigs on a vegetarian diet devoid of table scraps, you couldn't catch trichinosis from pork even if you ate it raw. Not that I'm trying to touch off a pork-sashimi fad, I'm just trying to reassure you that your pork is perfectly safe. The pork/trichinosis link lasted from the dawn of agriculture until the 1950s, when feeding garbage to pigs was banned in the United States. You are no more at risk of getting sick these days from eating undercooked pork than from eating any other undercooked meat—especially pork raised in the comfort and safety of your own home.

The risk of trichinosis, however, caused many old cookbooks to recommend cooking pork to an internal temperature of at least 170 degrees Fahrenheit. Anyone who has memories of eating pork chops the color and texture of worn shoe leather remembers these days vividly. Pork chops are a relatively lean cut of meat that dry out and toughen from overcooking; 170 degrees will cook the flavor (and the fun) right out of pork.

For those of you looking to cut it close the other way, here are the times and temperatures that USDA research has shown will kill Trichinae worms: six minutes at 131 degrees F, or one minute at 140 degrees. The key, of course, is making sure that the entire cut of meat reaches that temperature. The USDA recommends cooking pork to 160 degrees minimum, just to be safe.

But pork tastes much better at 150 degrees than at 160 degrees. Much, much better. Many gourmet chefs cook pork until the internal temperature reaches 145 degrees in the coldest part of the meat, knowing it will rise to 150 degrees while resting prior to carving. The result is delicious meat that is just slightly pink in the center.

 Above: Farmer Julie Brown put together a photo album of Cookie and her litter of fifteen piglets for visitors to see at North Hollow Farm.

Throw in the fact that most of your pork is going to be frozen prior to cooking and that freezing also kills Trichinae worms. The USDA research found that pork frozen to 5 degrees F for one hour also did the trick. So, in my view, eating your own pork is triply safe. I cook ours to 145 degrees, after having frozen it, after having raised it on a vegetarian diet. Oh my, is it good. If you've never eaten pink pork, you're never eaten tasty pork!

CHAPTER EIGHT

Financial Considerations

Let farmers furnish good fresh pork, and there will be found those who are willing to pay a liberal price for it.

—JOSEPH HARRIS

Pigs have become a major part of our small farm operation. I originally raised three pigs per year, mostly just for fun. This year, I'm raising ten pigs. As soon as I can figure out some larger pasture and housing arrangements, I hope to expand on that even more. The reason? Pigs pay. In addition to all the other wonderful attributes of pigs—their curiosity, their wide-ranging palate, their early-morning yawns—raising pigs can earn you a tidy profit. And that's even selling the animals whole, as I do, which is less profitable (but legally easier) than selling them by the pound.

As with any business enterprise, profit isn't guaranteed. It's possible to bungle even a seemingly sure thing. Then again, it's also possible to tease out a few loose bucks from an apparently losing proposition. One of the great compliments a Vermont farmer can pay you is to say that you can squeeze a nickel and come up with a dime.

Opposite: Tamworth/ Gloucestershire Old Spots piglets nurse from their mother at Hogwash Farm. The more pigs a farm raises for meat, the larger the potential profit.

How to successfully squeeze that nickel is what this chapter is all about. Keep in mind that, although I'm focusing on the dollar side of raising pigs, I'm still assuming that you are a backyarder

at heart and in it for the fun as much as for the money. Making a few bucks will be the lucky-strike extra.

I'm also assuming that you already own your own land (or are able to use someone else's land for free). Once you start talking about paying the mortgage with pigs, you're into a whole different league. This chapter isn't about quitting your day job and living high on the hog. It's about having a wonderful hobby or side business that pays its own way and then some.

To illustrate the potential profit and possible financial pitfalls of living with pigs, I've come up with two scenarios, based on the actual revenues

 Above: Cream, a Yorkshire sow, takes a nap in the lower level of the barn at North Hollow Farm. The farm's pigs are raised without growth stimulants or antibiotics and raised to a slaughter weight of 200 to 220 pounds.

and expenses that I've incurred in my most recent year of raising pigs. Some of these costs (grain, especially, it seems) will undoubtedly change over time, but these two scenarios will give you an idea of what to expect on the financial side of the ledger.

SCENARIO ONE: BREAK-EVEN

In a break-even scenario, you decide to raise two pigs. (Raising one pig is not recommended, as mentioned earlier, both because pigs are social animals and because one pig will not be motivated by friendly competition to eat and gain weight rapidly.) So you have two pigs. You buy them as six-week-old shoats in mid-May and raise them until mid-October. Let's say you have them for twenty weeks, or 140 days.

You don't have a whole lot of scrap wood lying around, and no access to free shipping pallets, so you buy a bunch of lumber and make a pen, trough, and shelter from scratch, buying a plastic water bucket, too. Since you aren't yet sold on raising pigs for the long term, you assume you're only in it for one year and need to recoup all the building costs right away.

Though you pay top dollar for the shoats, they end up not being especially vigorous or quick to gain weight. You call in the vet at one point to de-worm them, seeing as you have no livestock experience and aren't sure how to go about it, and hoping this will increase their weight gain. This is only partially successful. Despite the fact that you feed them store-bought grain almost exclusively, they only weigh 250 pounds each come slaughter day.

You load the finished hogs into your pickup truck and take them to the slaughterhouse, which charges you the usual amount for slaughter, butchering, and smoking the ham and bacon. It's an hour each way to the slaughterhouse, and you make two round trips—once to drop off the animals and once to pick up the meat.

All in all, you tally up ninety hours of work over the course of twenty weeks: twelve to build and set up the pen; four to go buy the shoats, bring them home, and get them safely installed; fifteen minutes, twice per day, to feed and water them; and four more hours on slaughter day.

In the end, you sell the hogs to two of your neighbors. Not wanting to gouge them on the price or worry that you're taking advantage of them, you settle on $3.25 per pound, hanging weight.

Above: A porcine pair struts its stuff at Luna Bleu Farm. The farm has been raising pigs for the past five years and produces food for one hundred families.

SCENARIO TWO: WE'RE IN THE MONEY

Before attaching dollars and cents to the details of scenario one, here's scenario two, which isn't that much different from scenario one in broad outline. You decide to raise three animals instead of two, since you have the space and lots of your friends are clamoring to buy your fresh, pasture-raised pork. You raise these animals for the same 140 days as in scenario one, though you shop around a bit and are able to buy the shoats for something less than top dollar.

You're also pretty good with a hammer and nails, and since you already have a fair bit of scrap wood lying around, you are able to tack together some pretty decent housing for not much cost. Also, since you know you're bullish on pigs, you're more than happy to spread the initial cost of construction over five years.

Your shoats are good ones, frolicking and snuffling and downing food at a prodigious rate. You buy them a bunch of grain to ensure good nutrition, but you also toss them a steady supply of spoiled vegetables and moldy bread that your local supermarket is glad to shovel your way. The pigs never seem to get wormy, and by the time slaughter day rolls around, your healthy hogs are weighing in at a rippling 280 pounds apiece.

You buy three quarts of vodka and do the slaughtering with your friend, who has experience with these details. You take the dressed sides to the butcher, who charges you the usual rate for butchering and smoking the hams and bacon. All in, you tally up ninety hours for scenario two: four for setting up the pen (it took you twenty, actually, the better part of a weekend, to build your Hog Heaven, but it's going to last five years), two for picking up the shoats and getting them safely acclimatized; fifteen minutes twice per day for food and water; and fourteen hours to slaughter the animals, deliver the sides to the butcher, and return later to pick up the meat.

In the end, with a bunch of your friends competing to buy your pigs, you push the market a bit and charge $3.75 per pound, hanging weight.

THE TWO SCENARIOS: REVENUE

As you can see, these two scenarios aren't that different from one another. You raise the pigs for the same amount of time. They live under similar conditions, and they eat similar types of food. It ends up being the small details and decisions that make the difference between breaking even and profitability.

Here is how the revenue breaks out for the two scenarios:

	Break-Even	Profitable
Number of pigs	2	3
Live weight at slaughter	200 pounds	280 pounds
Hanging weight	140 pounds	210 pounds
Sale price	$3.25/pound	$3.75/pound
Revenue per pig	$455	$787.50
Total revenue	$910	$2,362.50

You can immediately see how three small decisions ended up having a major impact on total revenue. The first was adding a third pig. It takes almost no incremental time to raise that third pig, since you're already going to be building the shelter and managing the food and water for the first two. You might as well do it for a third pig while you're at it (or a fourth . . .).

The second was buying healthy, vigorous shoats. I've exaggerated the difference between great shoats and not-so-great shoats to emphasize the point here, but you can see what a difference it can make. In the break-even scenario, the shoats just don't grow that well, and when they do grow, they end up being not well proportioned. In the profitable scenario, the pigs grow much larger, and a greater proportion of that size goes into pork.

The third minor decision that had a major impact on revenue was the sale price of the meat. Three twenty-five versus three-seventy-five doesn't seem like much, but when you multiply that extra fifty cents by the extra meat produced by the vigorous animals, you see a dramatic increase in

financial upside. Keep in mind that this is the price per hanging pound, which is how uninspected animals need to be legally sold.

You'll probably lose another 20 percent or so of weight during butchering, meaning that your $3.75 per pound hanging will translate into about $4.69 per pound of retail, packaged weight. What is your local market like? If your neighbors are accustomed to paying a premium for the highest-

quality, finest pork available, they might be willing to pay more than the equivalent of $4.69 per pound, even if they are required to buy the entire animal at once. Don't undersell your market—the pork you're raising is going to be as good as it gets, the best stuff in the world, and the flavor difference between homegrown, happy pork and the rather flaccid, gray stuff you get at the supermarket is more pronounced than for any other type of meat.

THE TWO SCENARIOS: EXPENSES

	Break-Even	Profitable
Price per shoat	$100.00	$75.00
Grain purchase, per hog	$96.00	$80.00
(50-LB. BAGS @ $8 PER BAG)	(12)	(10)
Vet visit for de-worming	$25.00	$0.00
Slaughter fee, per hog	$65.00	$15.00
	(SLAUGHTERHOUSE)	(VODKA PURCHASE)
Butchering, $0.55/pound	$77.00	$115.50
Smoking, $0.85/pound	$39.27	$58.91
(ROUGHLY ⅓ OF CARCASS)		
Total expenses, per hog	$402.27	$344.41
Total direct expenses, all hogs	$804.54	$1,033.23
Capital expenses	$100.00	$40.00
	($100 OVER 1 YEAR)	($200 OVER 5 YEARS)
Total all expenses	**$904.54**	**$1,073.23**

A quick review of these expenses shows that it cost only about $100 to raise that third pig, again thanks to the accumulation of a number of seemingly minor decisions. The first was buying the shoats for $75 instead of $100 each. The going rate in Vermont these days ranges from $50 to $100 each for spring shoats (when demand, and prices, are highest). I stay away from the $50 shoats, since they are generally of the medicated-feed, piglet-mill variety. In fact, I don't hesitate to pay $100 if the shoats are of the very highest quality. As we saw in the revenue calculation, a good shoat might produce more pork (several hundred dollars' worth) than a below-average one. Paying an extra $25 for a great shoat quickly turns into a bargain.

I also cut expenses by feeding the profitable hogs enough free food to cut back on the grain by 20 percent. Notice that I'm still feeding these hogs an awful lot of grain. I could save still more expense by feeding the pigs entirely on free food, but I'm convinced that the main reason our pork tastes so good is because the hogs eat primarily high-quality grain. Look at it

another way: If I fed no grain, I would have saved $80 per animal. But if I then could only charge $3.25 per pound for the pork, because the meat was good but not exceptional, I would have lost $105 on the revenue. That $80 in grain led to $25 in profit.

The use of outside experts also factored into the expense side. The wormy shoats together cost me a $50 vet bill. The slaughtering bill totaled $130. Learning how to de-worm pigs, either through liquid or injection, and taking the time to buy only high-quality shoats, quickly pays for itself. Learning how to slaughter does, too, though that may not be an area where you're willing or able to economize.

Finally, even though I plunked down $200 to fence and house the profitable hogs versus $100 for the break-even ones, I spread the $200 over fifteen pigs (three pigs per year for five years) and the $100 over only two pigs. That was the biggest line-item savings between the two scenarios.

THE TWO SCENARIOS: NET PROFIT

	Break-Even	Profitable
Gross revenue	$910.00	$2,362.50
Total expenses	$904.54	$1,073.23
Net profit	$5.46	$1,289.27
Hours worked	90	90
Hourly wage	$0.06	$14.33

Here's where the sum of these many, seemingly minor, decisions becomes obvious. In both scenarios, you put in about ninety hours of work over the course of five months. In the break-even scenario, you net a paltry five bucks for your effort, which works out to something like six cents per hour. In the profitable scenario, which required little more effort on your part, you netted thirteen hundred bucks, or nearly fourteen and a half dollars per hour.

EXTRA CREDIT: KEEPING A HOG FOR YOURSELF

In the above scenarios, I assumed that you sold all of your hogs to your friends and neighbors, keeping none for yourself. What are the chances of that happening? What are the chances of you watching all of that delicious, best-in-the-world pork end up on someone else's plate?

Pretty good, actually, if you have small children who've adopted your pen full of Wilburs over the course of the summer. It might be easier to explain that the Wilburs "went away on vacation" or "were sold to a nice farmer in the next county" rather than point to the chest freezer and say, "They're in there."

You'll need to be crafty. Keep in mind the opening scene of *Charlotte's Web*: When Fern sits down at the table after convincing her father to spare Wilbur's life, what does E. B. White have the family eating for breakfast? Bacon, of course. Don't worry—you'll find a way.

Let's look back at scenario two—the profitable scenario—for a second time, this time with you keeping the third pig for your own consumption. Raising that pig cost you about $384 in shoat purchase, grain, butchering-related expenses, and capital. Meanwhile, its sale brought you $788, for a net of $404.

Let's say you live in a state where payroll and income taxes take up 33 percent of your pretax income. In order to have that $384 on hand to pay for expenses, you'd actually have to go out and earn $574 at your day job and pay $190 in taxes in order to have that $384. So your pretax expenses are $574.

On the revenue side, let's say that, instead of keeping a pig for yourself, you went out and bought all that meat. At $788, and still assuming a 33 percent effective tax rate, you'd have to earn $1,175 at your day job and pay $387 in taxes in order to have that $788 on hand to buy the pork.

Perhaps you can see where this is going. In the actual case, you kept the meat for yourself, saving $1,175 in income you didn't have to go out and earn. You did have to pay all the expenses associated with that pig, however, which required you to earn $574. The net of these two is $601.

In other words, the two pigs that you sold to your neighbors netted you $430 apiece, or $860 total. The pig you kept for yourself netted $601. The all-three grand total, therefore, comes to $1,461. Divide that by the same ninety hours, and your wage is up to $16.24 per hour.

ENTER THE TAX MAN

Okay, I can already hear some of you screaming, "But you have to pay taxes on the net, so the savings goes away." True, true. But not so fast.

I've worked as a business manager at various times in my professional life and derive undue pleasure from taking seemingly straightforward numbers and twisting them around to cast a surprisingly favorable light on my farming enterprises. Lies, damn lies, and statistics, as the saying goes.

You do indeed need to pay taxes on the money you earn raising pigs— more on that in a moment. My point in taking the value of your keeper pig and turning it into its pretax value, in order to boost your perceived hourly wage, is this: When someone asks you how much money you make in your day job, do you ever answer with the post-tax amount? Of course not. You say, "Fifteen bucks an hour," not, "Eleven seventy-five after FICA and withholding."

Why should it be any different with your pigs? Apples to apples—give the pretax number: $16.24. You're not lying. You're just spinning it the way everyone else does.

FILING TAX FORMS—SCHEDULE F OR LINE 21

When it comes to paying the tax man, however, you can suddenly have it the other way. Since you didn't sell the third pig to anyone, you didn't earn any income on it. Your total income for the three pigs is $788 times two, or $1,576. Your expenses are still $1,073, which is what it cost to raise all three. Your net profit for taxes is $503.

This $503 needs to be reported on your federal income tax form and any other applicable state and local tax forms. There are two ways to go about doing this—Form 1040 Schedule F, if you plan on going into the business of raising pigs, or Line 21 on Form 1040, if you want your porcine adventures to remain a hobby.

The Internal Revenue Service (IRS) is rightly concerned about people setting up so-called "businesses" whose sole purpose is to lose money and shelter the rest of their income from taxation. For this reason, your pig-raising adventures will have to meet at least one of the following criteria in order for the IRS to consider it a legitimate business:

1. You must earn a profit in three years out of every five. If you do and are paying taxes on the profit, you're a business.

2. You need to act like a business. If you don't meet criteria #1, and end up being audited, you'll need to convince the authorities that you are, indeed, conducting an actual business. In other words, your business needs to be incorporated and registered with your state; you need to keep financial records and have a dedicated checking account for the

business; you should belong to relevant professional associations; and you should have a business plan in place that outlines your path toward profitability.

3. You need to be an active participant in the business. Even if you meet criteria #2, you should also meet this criteria as well by having documentation that shows you working at least one hundred hours per year in the business, and that the investment in the business is yours, not someone else's.

If you meet either criteria #1 or a combination of #2 and #3, you should file Form 1040 Schedule F—Profit or Loss from Farming, to report your income and expenses. You'll be a bona fide farmer in the eyes of the IRS.

You may also be much further into the business world than you ever wanted to be. If your thoughts while reading the previous paragraphs were something along the lines of, "For crying out loud—I just wanted to raise a few pigs!" you should follow a much simpler route: Report your net income on Line 21 of Form 1040, the "other income" line.

Line 21 is where you report hobby income or other taxable income that is not part of a business or salaried job. Write in your $503 net profit, add a note to the effect of "income from raising pigs," and leave it at that. If you end up losing money next year, no biggie—there's nothing to report. If you take a few years off between sounders of shoats, the IRS won't blink an eye. You're not a business and are free to come and go as you please, making money or losing it to your heart's content.

No tax discussion is complete without the usual disclaimer: This is a book about raising pigs for fun and profit, not about correctly filling out tax forms. You should check with your qualified tax professional (I love that—implying that we all have a qualified tax professional at our beck and call!) before filing your own tax forms. The discussion of who is a business and who isn't, and who ought to be and who oughtn't, can fill many volumes of tax law. Especially if you're considering raising pigs as part of a larger agricultural enterprise, or are thinking of going for it big-time, you should seek professional help (double entendre not unintentional).

CHAPTER NINE

The Health of Your Pigs

The great point in the management of young pigs is, to keep them growing rapidly. If strong and vigorous, they are seldom liable to any disease, and if attacked, soon throw it off.

—JOSEPH HARRIS

This is going to be a short chapter. Yet another great thing about living with pigs: no vet bills.

Here are the two keys to raising healthy pigs: buy healthy shoats (a topic treated in great detail in chapter 1), and raise them outside (a topic covered in chapters 3 and 5). Provided you do that, and provided you take care of the obvious stuff like fresh water, good food, and pleasant living conditions, your pigs will be healthy as horses.

Scratch that—much healthier than horses. When I was a kiddo, my parents used to say: "Drink your milk; you'll grow up to be as healthy as a horse." Given what I now know about equine care and feeding, with the vet bills and the farrier bills and the careful attention to feeding, I wish they'd promised me a life as healthy as a hog. The only mention of pigs that I recall from childhood had something to do with the living conditions in my bedroom.

Nevertheless, there are a few things for you to keep in mind in the veterinary line as you embark upon life with pigs. Chief among these is poop.

Opposite: Nancy LaRowe gives her Tamworth boar Lug a pat while visiting it in the pasture at Hogwash Farm. The secret to healthy hogs is a combination of fresh water, good food, and pleasant living conditions.

THE POOP ON POOP

One of the best indicators of your pigs' health is the consistency of their manure. Poop from healthy pigs has the texture of a soft mash, sort of like soft polenta or overcooked Irish oatmeal. (I love oatmeal—no offense intended. Same with polenta.) It loosely holds together into a turd shape, at least while fresh, before collapsing into an amorphous pile. You'll come to know it (and appreciate it) when you see it.

If your pigs' excrement is more like runny liquid, especially for several days on end (and not related to some particularly pungent pile of rancid yogurt you scored from a Dumpster), you have a problem.

I usually encounter this when I first bring the shoats home in the spring, when they've just been weaned. The change in diet, coupled with the stress of changed circumstances, often gives the little guys the runs. The solution is dirt.

One year, a combination of late snowstorms and an early farrowing meant that I had to keep my shoats in the barn for three weeks before moving them out on pasture. The poor little guys—they were all guys—had good cases of diarrhea. I called up the breeder to ask for advice, and she said, "Get them outside and into the dirt. It will clear them right up." I did, and it did. The wild pig is an earth-eating machine, and something about the grit, the microbes, and the roughage of dirt seems crucial to healthy pig digestion.

If your shoats (or hogs) are living in a tiny sty where the manure is getting ankle-deep and attracting flies, they effectively won't have access to fresh dirt. My first advice is to make a much larger pen for them so that they can establish a latrine area away from their feeding area. My second is to shovel out that manure on a regular basis, mix it with a leavening agent (straw, sawdust, or wood chips are good), and compost it a safe distance away. Pigs forced to live in their own manure will likely become sick pigs.

If your adult hogs come down with the runs, however, it's not weaning and stress that you're up against; it's probably worms.

 Above: Laverne the Yorkshire cross gets a snout full of dirt at Sunrise Farm. The key to healthy digestion for shoats is access to fresh dirt.

DE-WORMING A PIG

Most of the years we've had pigs, I haven't had to de-worm them. Provided the shoats have come from a reputable breeder, who keeps clean facilities and who de-worms the shoats just before you pick them up, and provided you keep your animals outside in a reasonably

sized pen, you should have no worm issues. Nevertheless, a few times I've had to de-worm my pigs.

Since I keep sheep as well as pigs, and already have a supply of syringes and de-wormer on hand, I elect to go the injectable de-wormer route. Before feeding the pigs one afternoon, I load my pocket with one syringe for each animal. Then I slop down the grain and greens and do my custom-

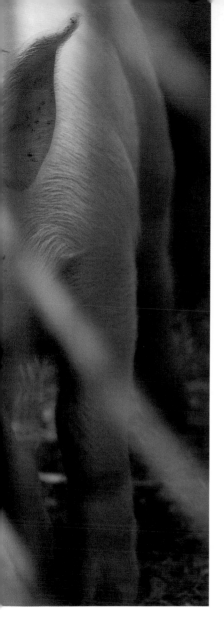

Above: Yorkshire piglets from separate litters take a look at each other at North Hollow Farm.

ary rub of each animal's neck and back. Only this time, while I am rubbing the haunches, I quickly fire an injection into the rump. Each pig lets out a squeak of surprise, but looking around and seeing nothing amiss (my hand is already back into my pocket), returns to feeding. No problem.

The two keys to this approach are preparation and confidence. Make sure the syringe is loaded with exactly the right dose (the label will list dosage versus animal weight). Grip the syringe in between your thumb and second finger, with your first finger on the plunger. Find a good piece of muscular haunch, where the flesh is sure to be deeper than your needle is long (I use a 1-inch needle, 14-gauge). Then dart the needle into the pig's butt, your thumb and second finger driving the needle in, with your first finger following through on the plunger once the syringe hits bottom. It's a two-part motion that happens almost simultaneously, a *ka-thwack*, where the *ka* is the syringe darting in and the *thwack* is your finger plunging in the dose. Don't be slow, don't be gentle, don't be cautious. Just go for it—in and out. Then hide the syringe, rubbing the pig's back as if nothing at all out of the ordinary has just happened. ("Who me? I didn't see nothing.") Then casually move on to the next pig.

I've read that injecting into the front shoulder is less painful for the pig, and I keep meaning to go that route, but two things stop me: The ham is such a big and obvious target, and my

Above: A sow enjoys playing with a sawdust bag after Jennifer Megyesi emptied it for new bedding at Fat Rooster Farm.

pigs haven't seemed very pained by being stuck in the rump. But one of these years, I'll try the shoulder.

If firing syringes into hams or shoulders isn't what you have in mind, you can also buy a liquid de-wormer that you add to the drinking water and let the pigs drink. Much easier, though much less dramatic. Also much harder to impress your friends. Check in at your local feed store for advice on which de-wormer works best in your area, or check the Tools and Equipment listing in the appendix of this book.

Two other thoughts on de-worming: First, as I said before, you won't ever need to do it as long as your shoats were de-wormed by the breeder and your pigs have access to fresh ground. Second, most de-wormers require at least a four-week "withdrawal period" before the pigs are to be slaughtered. Make sure you have plenty of time to spare—six to eight weeks is better. You don't want to be marring your unbelievably good, pasture-raised pork with residual medication.

WHEN TO CALL THE VET

Beyond worms, there's very little that might go wrong with an otherwise healthy hog. But there's also not much you can do about many health problems, at least economically. Having a vet come work on a sick pig is expensive, and unless the pig in question is a sow or boar with potential future earning power, it's not likely to be something you can (or want to) afford. Here is where you'll discover how far you've gone in starting to think of your pigs as pets. A $300 vet bill seems easier to justify for the family dog; what about when it's for a hog with only six weeks left to live and a potential profit of only $250?

A quick rule of thumb: Pigs that are eating are pigs that don't require veterinary care. A pig that doesn't get up to eat, or a pig that is listless, or a pig whose normally bright, shining eyes are small and beady, is a pig that's not well.

One year, we bought four shoats from something of a "piglet mill"—a farm that churns out piglets in mass quantity. The price was right, or so I thought. Two of the four ended up having hernias, and one of the two had an endless series of ailments, from an ear that puffed up around an infected ear tag, to a front hoof that couldn't bear weight, to a case of raspy breathing that eventually turned into nightly snoring that could be heard 100 yards away. (The amplification under the metal roof of the shelter helped with the acoustics.)

I called the vet. She laid out the options, which included injectable antibiotics, a farm visit, and a few other steps that were going to run into three figures. "Is he still eating?" she asked. When I answered in the affirmative, she said, "Call me back if he stops eating."

Well, he never stopped eating. His ailments came and went. He was obviously not a pig with a robust immune system, and except for the hernia, which swelled into a softball-sized orb under his abdomen, and the snoring, which increased in profundity as his lungs gained size and strength over the months, he grew out of everything else. Clean water, good food, and fresh dirt kept him going.

If a pig does stop eating and declines to get up at feeding time, your first step, before calling the vet, should be to take its temperature. Insert a thermometer three inches into the pig's rectum to get an accurate reading. An ordinary human thermometer is fine (though you might want to retire it to the barn afterward). Tie or tape a piece of string to the thermometer so that you have a handle in case the pig jumps up and the thermometer falls out.

I've actually never had to take a pig's temperature. One time I approached a downed pig, thermometer in hand, but as I maneuvered the thermometer into place, the pig shot up and gave me a nasty glance. Apparently he wasn't that sick after all. He ambled over to the feeder, and though he led a healthy life thereafter, I felt that our relationship never fully recovered.

If your pig is sick enough that you are able to take its temperature, 102 degrees F is the magic number for a healthy pig. (Actually, anything between 101.6 F and 103.6 F is in the normal range.) If you're above the range, your pig is trying to fight something off. If you're below the range, your pig may be in the process of giving up, making time of the essence. Either way, call your vet in the very unlikely case that matters get this far out of hand.

I want to end this chapter on a bright note, and, as promised, keep it short. I will say this: Sick pigs have been an aberration for us, and ones that could have been entirely avoided by buying healthy shoats in the first place. So, that's my advice: Buy a healthy shoat and forget about this chapter altogether.

A FINAL NOTE: NOSE RINGS

Although it's not common in the world of backyard pig raising, sooner or later you're apt to come across a suggestion that you put rings in your pigs' noses. Your shoat supplier may even offer to do it for you. The purpose of the ring is to prevent your pig from rooting in the dirt and tearing up the sod. The ring has sharp ends that cut into the pig's snout when under pressure.

Above: Frannie, a four-and-a-half-month-old hog, roams in a wintery barnyard at Luna Bleu Farm in South Royalton, VT.

I strongly recommend that you not put rings in your pigs' noses. Pigs live for their noses. Watch them; it's what they do—snuffling into things, rooting around under things, sticking their noses into holes and digging up dirt. Depriving pigs of this most piggish of sensations is depriving them of the essence of what it means to be a pig. What you're left with is a pork-producing organism, which is not nearly so fun (for you or the animal) as an actual pig.

If your concern is not having your pigs root up your lawn, put their pen somewhere where it's fine for them to go digging. Just don't put rings in their noses. It may be all the rage in the teenage set these days, but it's going out of style among the porcine crowd.

APPENDIX ONE

Pigs in Literature

One great way to further your appreciation of all things pig is to read about your porcine companions. (This will happen at night, presumably, after you've tucked them in with a fresh bucket of slops and have some time on your hands.) Pigs seem to make the leap from barnyard to bookstore more often than just about any other creature except the trusty dog. This is no doubt because the pig is such a marvelous and multilayered metaphor, apt for any number of occasions. Here are a few favorites:

The **Three Little Pigs** fairy tale

The **Freddy the Pig** series, by Walter R. Brooks

Winnie-the-Pooh and **The House at Pooh Corner**, by A. A. Milne

The Good Good Pig, by Sy Montgomery

Animal Farm, by George Orwell

A Day No Pigs Would Die, by Robert Newton Peck

Chester, the Wordly Pig, by Bill Peet

The Tale of Pigling Bland and **The Tale of Little Pig Robinson**, by Beatrix Potter

Charlotte's Web, by E. B. White

Blandings Castle series of novels and stories, by P. G. Wodehouse

 Opposite: Zola the Tamworth piglet greets Chi Chi the Large Black and Tamworth sow in the pasture at Hogwash Farm. Fenced with portable fencing and housed in portable huts, the pigs regularly rotate between pastures.

APPENDIX TWO

List of Tools and Equipment

One of the great advantages of living with pigs is that very little is required in the way of specialized tools and equipment. Most every aspect of pig care, from housing to fencing to food and water, can be handled with improvisation and making use of whatever materials you happen to have at hand. Nevertheless, a few words on the subject are in order, since some materials work better than others.

CHAPTER 1: BUYING PIGLETS

Breeds. Oklahoma State University maintains a wonderful website with the photographs and brief histories of more than fifty varieties of pigs. If you're trying to decide on a breed, or merely want to be astonished at the wide range of colors and shapes that pigs come in, go to http://www.ansi.okstate.edu/breeds/swine.

CHAPTER 2: THE FIRST FEW WEEKS

Shelter. An inexpensive and easy way to build a pen for your shoats' first few weeks is to nail together wooden shipping pallets. Many large retail stores, and even agricultural feed stores, are likely to have a few extras that they'd be happy to have you take off their hands. Short of that, sheets of 4x8 CDX (the inexpensive kind) plywood work beautifully.

Transportation. Good options for transporting shoats around are large, rugged cardboard boxes that are in good shape.

Opposite: At left, Hank, a boar on loan from The Mountain School of Milton Academy in Vershire, VT, tries to get a bit of grain while sharing a pen with Flo the sow at Luna Bleu Farm.

Appliance boxes tend to work the best because they're already designed for holding heavy weight. Plastic or metal dog crates also work well and are often for sale, used, through the classifieds. If you end up using a metal-lattice cage, drape or tie a towel or sheet around all sides but one so that the shoats don't feel too exposed during transit.

Bedding. Your shoats will love to burrow down into something for sleeping, which helps the little guys stay warm and feel safe. Straw is ideal for this, since it's clean and dry, but most any hay will work well, provided it isn't wet and moldy. Shovel it out every few days or so and replace with fresh.

Manure management. A metal wheelbarrow and old, flat-bottomed shovel are ideal for managing manure during the shoats' first few weeks. The animals won't be producing large quantities of poop, but you'll still want to clean their pen every day or so. Metal beats plastic for this task because it won't retain odors after being rinsed out.

Feeding. Since your shoats are fresh from an all-milk diet, you'll want to feed them wet and runny food at this stage of life. I've used everything from an old oven pan to a trash can lid to a rubber feeder tub for holding their food. The rubber tub works best, the kind with the 2-inch sides, because the shoats can bump into it without tipping it over. The high-sided tubs (6 inches or more) are too difficult for the shoats to access. Your local feed store should have these in a range of sizes.

Water. Here again, a rubber bucket is best since it flexes and is less likely to spill by accident. I like the kind that's about 8 inches tall, with a metal handle that I can tie to the sides of the pen to keep it from spilling.

CHAPTER 3: WHERE YOUR PIGS WILL LIVE

Tarp. If you live in a warm, relatively dry climate, a simple tarp (available at your hardware store) stretched between trees works beautifully.

Building shelters. There are many wonderful books in print on how to build farm buildings. Try a Web search on "building a pole barn" to get yourself started.

Portable shelters. The design in this chapter is for an 8x16-foot wooden shelter on skids, which will house four to five pigs through a season. You can also try a Web search on "portable pig shelters," which will turn up other designs as well as prefabricated steel shelters that are shipped to you with some assembly required.

CHAPTER 4: WHAT YOUR PIGS WILL EAT

Feeders. The design in this chapter is for a wooden trough that your pigs can easily access yet have trouble flipping over. Your local feed store will also carry plastic, metal, or rubber feeders that sit on the ground. If you're interested in a more elaborate self-feeding system, try a Web search on "hog self-feeder."

Grain. Your local feed store will carry some sort of commercial grain mix for hogs, and most anything non-medicated should be fine. *Buckets.* Whether for soaking grain before

feeding or for carrying water, the ubiquitous 5-gallon plastic "Sheetrock" bucket is ideal.

Watering. Five-gallon buckets hung from the pen wall will work as a simple watering solution, especially if outfitted with watering nipples. You local feed store will also carry a variety of plastic and rubber options.

Watering nipples. These are a great solution for situations where you don't want to be wasting water. Search the Web under "pig nipple" if your feed store doesn't carry any. Be sure to buy the nipples that are designed for buckets, not water pipes, since they have a flange to hold a washer against the bucket. Once you have the nipples in hand, go to your local hardware store to buy washers and the 1/2-inch pipe fitting needed to secure it to the bucket. Mount three of these in a 5-gallon Sheetrock bucket for an ideal three- to six-pig waterer.

CHAPTER 5: FENCING

Hog panels. These sections of welded metal fencing are sold at most farm-supply stores. They typically come in 8-foot and 16-foot lengths, and in 34-inch and 48-inch heights. Secure them using 6-foot metal T-posts every 4 feet.

Electric wire. Most farm-supply stores also sell electric wire, with the braided metal/plastic "electric rope" being easier to work with than the all-metal wire (which is difficult to keep tight or roll back up).

Portable netting. If you decide to use electric netting instead of metal wires, be sure to buy the type with the plastic vertical spacers that prevent sagging. Try the website www.premier1supplies.com, and look at the ElectroNet sheep fencing to get an idea of what you're looking for. There are two tricks to remember when handling netting. First, when paying it out, walk backwards so that your feet won't get tangled in the netting. Second, when picking it up, don't roll it. Instead, gather all the posts in one hand as you go, letting the netting hang down between them. When you have it all in hand, lay it on the ground and roll the netting up to the posts. This will prevent tangles next time you pay it out.

Charger. Buy a charger that uses high-voltage pulses rather than continuous current. High-voltage pulses are less dangerous to humans, require less electricity, don't melt portable netting, and do a better job combating weeds. Solar-powered charges are commonly available these days and are a good solution if you don't have ready access to AC power. Because the solar kit costs a fair bit, however, I'd recommend using an AC model if it's at all convenient.

Grounding rods. Buy copper grounding rods at your local hardware store for grounding the charger and fence. The charger will have instructions for how to properly install them.

Lightning choke. I didn't install a lightning choke until after my first charger had been burnt to a crisp. Too bad—the choke costs $20, and the charger $200. Buy a lightning choke from a national supplier if your local store doesn't carry them, and be sure to follow the directions exactly. When properly installed, the choke will prevent a nearby lightning strike from going through your fence and damaging the charger (and possibly your home's electrical supply).

Feed cable. You'll want at least a short length of shielded cable for running the electricity from the charger to the fence. This is also handy for running the charge underneath gates and anywhere else human hands are likely to be fumbling.

CHAPTER 6: SLAUGHTER DAY

Hog weigh tape. If you don't want to use a regular tape measure and do the math, purchase one of these handy weigh tapes at your feed store, or search the Web for "hog weigh tape."

Transportation. Remember that hogs ready for slaughter are huge, strong, and likely to be in bad humor if you're trying to corral them into an unfamiliar vehicle. Make sure all your chutes and ramps are made from stout lumber and that there are no openings that might cause your hogs to try to make a break for it.

Vodka. If you decide to do it yourself, figure on a quart of vodka per hog. No need to use anything but the cheap stuff.
Hose and scrub brushes. Almost any old brush will do. Use a nozzle on the hose to make rinsing easier.

An 8-inch kitchen knife. This is for cutting the jugular, so you want something strong that you can stick straight into the neck. A thinner, more flexible blade might not be adequate for the task.

Skinning or paring knife, one per person. I keep meaning to buy a skinning knife but have been slowed down by the fact that an ordinary paring knife works pretty well. These need to be kept very sharp, so have a stone or sharpening tool on hand for frequent touch-ups.

Sharp hatchet or ax. This is for splitting the pelvis, especially on an older hog where the bone is too hard to cut easily. Alternatively, use short pieces of string to tie off the urethra and rectum and pass them through the pelvis.

Tractor with bucket. Being able to lift the carcass off the ground, either using a tractor or winch-and-tripod system, makes it possible to keep the meat much cleaner than having to do everything on the ground.

Length of chain with cinch ring on one end. This is useful for grabbing the carcass by one leg and hoisting it off the ground while it bleeds out

Handgun or rifle. As mentioned in the chapter, a .22-gauge rifle is adequate for the job, assuming you know exactly what you're doing. Otherwise, a larger-caliber handgun leaves more margin for error.

One gambrel or set of hooks for each pig. If you don't have a butcher-supply store nearby, try a Web search on "hog hooks" or "hog gambrel" to get an idea of what's available. Since you'll be splitting the carcasses, use either separate hooks or a gambrel that can hold one side at a time.

A 3- to 4-foot, sturdy, v-shaped sawhorse. You can build this yourself using locally bought lumber. Build it tall enough so that you can work on the carcass at a convenient height.

Reciprocating saw or butcher's handsaw. If you don't have a butcher's saw (and don't want to buy one specially), a Sawzall®-type reciprocating saw works fine. Use a wood blade and disinfect it before and afterward.

Contractor-grade trash bags. These are made from 6-mil plastic and are tall enough to hold an entire side for transportation to the butcher, if needed.

Barrels or trash cans. Metal is better than plastic, since it won't retain odors.

CHAPTER 8: FINANCIAL CONSIDERATIONS

Recordkeeping. The secret to making money raising pigs is to keep good records; the secret to keeping good records is making it easy to do so. Designate a folder in a file cabinet or even label a cardboard shoebox in the corner of your kitchen. Throw in all the paperwork as you go—receipts, expenses, notes on telephone conversations, anything that will remind you of what happened when—so that you can add it all up at the end of the year. If you have such a folder or shoebox, your recordkeeping will be straightforward. If not, you'll be amazed at how quickly you forget important details.

CHAPTER 9: THE HEALTH OF YOUR PIGS

De-worming liquid. Your feed store is likely to carry the liquid de-wormer that you can mix in with the drinking water. If not, search the Web for "hog de-wormer."

De-worming syringe and needles. Again, if your feed store doesn't carry this equipment, try a "hog de-wormer" Web search. Buy an injectable de-worming liquid designed for hogs, along with some disposable syringes and package of 14-gauge, 1-inch disposable needles.

Thermometer. Any old human thermometer will do—just be sure to label it for porcine use only afterward and keep it with your pig equipment. Tie or tape on a foot or so of string to make it easier to retrieve if your pig decides to get up and walk away mid-procedure.

Above: Two shoats inspect fresh bedding at Fat Rooster Farm.

APPENDIX THREE

State Cooperative Extension Offices

For a national overview of cooperative extension programs, visit the United States Department of Agriculture Web site at www.csrees.usda.gov/Extension/index.html.

Alabama
Alabama Cooperative Extension System
109-D Duncan Hall
Auburn University, AL 36849
Tel: (334) 844–4444
www.aces.edu

Alaska
University of Alaska Fairbanks
Cooperative Extension Service
P.O. Box 756180
Fairbanks, AK 99775
Tel: (907) 474–7188
www.alaska.edu/uaf/ces

Arizona
University of Arizona
Cooperative Extension, Forbes 301
P.O. Box 210036
Tucson, AZ 85721-0036
Tel: (520) 621–7205
www.ag.arizona.edu/extension

Arkansas
University of Arkansas
Division of Agriculture
Cooperative Extension Service
2301 South University Avenue
Little Rock, AK 72204
Tel: (501) 671–2000
www.uaex.edu

California
University of California
Agriculture and Natural Resources
Cooperative Extension
Tel: (530) 752–1250
http://ucanr.org/ce.cfm

Colorado
Colorado State University Extension
1311 S. College Building—University Avenue
Fort Collins, CO 80523-4040
Tel: (970) 491–1321
www.ext.colostate.edu/index.html

Connecticut
University of Connecticut
Cooperative Extension System
W. B. Young Building, Room 231
1376 Storrs Road, Unit 4134
Storrs, Connecticut 06269-4134
Tel: (860) 486–9228
www.extension.uconn.edu

Delaware
University of Delaware
College of Agriculture and Natural Resources
Cooperative Extension, Townsend Hall
531 South College Avenue
Newark, Delaware 19716-2103
Tel: (800) 282–8685
http://ag.udel.edu/extension/index.php

Opposite: A hog scarfs every last bit of grain from the pail at Luna Bleu Farm.

Florida
University of Florida
IFAS Cooperative Extension
P.O. Box 110210
Gainesville, FL 32611
Tel: (352) 392–1761
http://solutionsforyourlife.ufl.edu

Georgia
University of Georgia
College of Agriculture and Environmental
Sciences
Cooperative Extension
Tel: (800) ASK–UGA1
www.ugaextension.com

Hawaii
University of Hawaii
College of Tropical Agriculture and Human
Resources
Cooperative Extension Service
3050 Maile Way, Gilmore 203
Honolulu, HI 96822
Tel: (808) 956–8139
www.ctahr.hawaii.edu/site/Extprograms.aspx

Idaho
Director of Cooperative Extension
University of Idaho at Twin Falls
P.O. Box 1827
Twin Falls, ID 83303-1827
Tel: (208) 736–3603
www.extension.uidaho.edu

Illinois
University of Illinois Extension
Office of Extension and Outreach
214 Mumford Hall (MC-710)
1301 W. Gregory Drive
Urbana, IL 61801
Tel: (217) 333–5900
http://web.extension.uiuc.edu/state/
index.html

Indiana
Purdue University Extension
Animal Science Department
1151 Lilly Hall
West Lafayette, IN 47906
Tel: (888) 398–4636
www.ces.purdue.edu/counties.htm

Iowa
Iowa State University
University Extension
2150 Beardshear
Ames, IA 50011
Tel: (515) 294–6675
www.extension.iastate.edu

Kansas
Kansas State University
228 Weber Hall
Manhattan, KS 66506-0201
Tel: (785) 532–5790
www.oznet.ksu.edu

Kentucky
University of Kentucky
College of Agriculture
S-107 Ag. Sciences Building, North
Lexington, KY 40546
Tel: (859) 257–4302
http://ces.ca.uky.edu/ces

Louisiana
Louisiana State University
Agricultural Center
101 Efferson Hall
P.O. Box 25203
Baton Rouge, LA 70803
Tel: (225) 578–4161
www.lsuagcenter.com/en/our_offices/
parishes

Maine
University of Maine Cooperative Extension
Animal, Veterinary, and Aquatic Sciences
Office
332 Hitchner Hall
Orono, ME 04469-5735
Tel: (207) 581–2787
www.umext.maine.edu/Default.htm

Maryland
University of Maryland
College of Agriculture and Natural Resources
1413A—AnSc/AgEn Building
College Park, MD 20742
Tel: (301) 405–1366
http://extension.umd.edu

Massachusetts
Agriculture and Landscape Extension
French Hall
230 Stockbridge Road
University of Massachusetts
Amherst, MA 01003-9316
Tel: (413) 545–0895
www.umassextension.org

Michigan
Michigan State University Extension
108 Agriculture Hall, Room 108
Michigan State University
East Lansing, MI 48824
Tel: (517) 355–2308
www.msue.msu.edu/portal/default.cfm?
pageset_id=25744&page_id=25770&msue_
portal_id=25643

Minnesota
University of Minnesota Extension Service
240 Coffey Hall
1420 Eckles Avenue
St. Paul, MN 55108-6068
Tel: (612) 624–1222
www.extension.umn.edu

Mississippi
Mississippi State University
P.O. Box 9601
Mississippi State, MS 39762
Tel: (601) 325–3036
http://msucares.com

Missouri
University of Missouri
College of Agriculture
2-28 Agriculture Building
Columbia, MO 65211
Tel: (573) 882–6385
http://extension.missouri.edu

Montana
MSU Extension
Montana State University
203 Culbertson
P.O. Box 172230
Bozeman, MT 59717
Tel: (406) 994–1750
http://extn.msu.montana.edu

Nebraska
University of Nebraska Extension
211 Agriculture Hall
Lincoln, NE 68583
Tel: (402) 472–2966
www.extension.unl.edu

Nevada
University of Nevada
Cooperative Extension
Reno MS 404
Reno, NV 89557
Tel: (775) 784–7070
www.unce.unr.edu

New Hampshire
UNH Cooperative Extension
200 Bedford Street (Mill #3)
Manchester, NH 03101
Tel: (877) 398–4769
http://extension.unh.edu

New Jersey
Rutgers, The State University of New Jersey
Cooperative Extension Service
88 Lipman Drive
New Brunswick, NJ 08901
Tel: (732) 932–7000 ext. 4204
http://njaes.rutgers.edu

New Mexico
New Mexico State University
Extension Animal Sciences
Knox Hall, Room 232
P.O. Box 30003 MSC 3AE
Las Cruces, NM 88003
Tel: (505) 646–3326
www.cahe.nmsu.edu

New York
Cornell University
Cooperative Extension
Box 26—Kennedy Hall
Ithaca, NY 14853
Tel: (607) 255–0789
www.cce.cornell.edu

North Carolina
North Carolina A&T State University
Coltrane Hall
Greensboro, NC 27411
Tel: (336) 334–7956
www.ag.ncat.edu/extension

North Dakota
North Dakota State University
Extension Service
Morrill Hall 315
Fargo, ND 58105
Tel: (701) 231–8944
www.ext.nodak.edu

Ohio
Ohio State University
Cooperative Extension
2120 Fyffe Road, Room 3
Columbus, OH 43210
Tel: (612) 292–6181
http://extension.osu.edu

Oklahoma
Oklahoma State University
Cooperative Extension Service
Division of Agricultural Sciences
136 Ag Hall
Stillwater, OK 74078
Tel: (405) 744–5398
www.oces.okstate.edu

Oregon
Oregon State University
Extension Service Administration
101 Ballard Hall
Corvallis, OR 97331
Tel: (541) 737–2713
http://extension.oregonstate.edu

Pennsylvania
Pennsylvania State University
Cooperative Extension Service
217 Ag Administration Building
University Park, PA 16802
Tel: (814) 865–5410
www.extension.psu.edu

Rhode Island
University of Rhode Island
Cooperative Extension
Fisheries/Animal/Vet Science Department
210B Woodward Hall
Kingston, RI 02881
Tel: (401) 874–2900
www.uri.edu/ce/index1.html

South Carolina
Clemson University
Cooperative Extension
103 Barre Hall
Clemson, SC 29634-0110
Tel: (864) 656–3382
http://virtual.clemson.edu/groups/extension

South Dakota
South Dakota State University
Cooperative Extension Service
AGH 154 / Box 2207D
Brookings, SD 57007
Tel: (605) 688–4892
http://sdces.sdstate.edu

Tennessee
University of Tennessee
Extension Service
2621 Morgan Circle
121 Morgan Hall
Knoxville, TN 37996
Tel: (865) 974–7114
www.utextension.utk.edu/default.asp

Texas
Texas A & M University
Cooperative Extension Service
Room 112—Williams Administration
7101 TAMU
College Station, TX 77843
Tel: (979) 845–7800
http://texasextension.tamu.edu

Utah
Utah State University
Extension Service
Animal, Dairy, and Veterinary Sciences
4815 Main Hill
Logan, UT 84322
Tel: (435) 797–2162
http://extension.usu.edu

Vermont
University of Vermont
Extension Service
19 Roosevelt Highway, Suite 305
Colchester, VT 05446
Tel: (802) 656–2990
www.uvm.edu/~uvmext

Virginia
Virginia Tech
Cooperative Extension Service
101 Hutcheson Hall (Mail Code 0402)
Blacksburg, VA 24061
Tel: (540) 231–5299
www.ext.vt.edu

Washington
Washington State University
Extension Service
P.O. Box 646248
Hulbert 411
Pullman, WA 99164-6248
Tel: (509) 335–2837
http://ext.wsu.edu

West Virginia
West Virginia University
Extension Service
P.O. Box 6031
Morgantown, WV 26506
Tel: (304) 293–5691
www.wvu.edu/~exten

Wisconsin
University of Wisconsin Extension
Agriculture and Natural Resources
277 Animal Sciences Building
1675 Observatory Drive
Madison, WI 53706
Tel: (608) 263–7320
www.uwex.edu/ces

Wyoming
University of Wyoming
Cooperative Extension Service
Department 3354
1000 E. University Avenue
Laramie, WY 82071
Tel: (307) 766–5124
http://ces.uwyo.edu

APPENDIX FOUR

State Pork Associations

Not every state has a pork association, but the ones listed here may serve as helpful sources of information about breeds suited to your area, equipment, community programs and resources, environmental regulations, and more.

Alabama Pork Producers
P.O. Box 11000
2108 East South Boulevard
Montgomery, AL 36191
Tel: (800) 392–5705
www.alabamaporkproducers.org

Arizona Pork Council
1102 E. Avenida Grande
Casa Grande, AZ 85222-1004
Tel: (520) 836–0050

Arkansas Pork Producers Association
625 Buck Mountain Road
Dover, AR 72837
Tel: (877) 444–7675
www.arpork.org

California Pork Producers Association
1225 H Street, Suite 106
Sacramento, CA 95814
Tel: (916) 447–8950
www.calpork.com

Colorado Pork Producers Council
822 7th Street, Suite 210
Greeley, CO 80631
Tel: (970) 378–0500 ext. 12

Delaware Pork Producers Association
27701 James Road
Laurel, DE 19956-2502
Tel: (302) 875–9079

Florida Pork Improvement Group
5700 SW 34th Street
Gainesville, FL 32608-5300
Tel: (352) 374–1542

Georgia Pork Producers Association
100 Miller Street
Camilla, GA 31730
Tel: (229) 336–7760
www.gapork.org

Hawaii Pork Industry Association
4173 Noho Road
Koloa, HI 96756
Tel: (808) 742–7285

Idaho Pork Producers Association
867 N. White Barn Road
Kuna, ID 83634
Tel: (208) 898–0454

Opposite: A young piglet roots through old corn stalks at The Reimanis Farm. "We raise pigs because we love them," said Kate Reimanis. "They are very smart animals, they are relatively easy to care for, they stay healthy and heal well from injuries, and we like scratching their backs."

Illinois Pork Producers Association
6411 S. Sixth Street Road
Springfield, IL 62712-6817
Tel: (217) 529–3100
www.ilpork.com

Indiana Pork Producers Association
4649 Northwestern Drive
Zionsville, IN 46077-9248
Tel: (800) 535–2405
www.indianapork.com

Iowa Pork Producers Association
1636 NW 114th Street
Clive, IA 50325-7071
Tel: (800) 372–7675
www.iowapork.org

Kansas Pork Association
2601 Farm Bureau Road
Manhattan, KS 66502-3066
Tel: (785) 776–0442
www.kspork.org

Kentucky Pork Producers Association
1110 Hawkins Drive
Elizabethtown, KY 42701-0607
Tel: (270) 737–5665

Louisiana Pork Producers Association
319 W. Claude Street
Lake Charles, LA 70605
Tel: (337) 475–5691
www.laporkproducers.com

Maine Hog Growers Association
161 Souther Road
Livermore Falls, ME 04254-4227
Tel: (207) 897–3706
www.katahdinoutdoors.com/mainepork

Maryland Pork Producers Association
53 Slama Road
Edgewater, MD 21037-1423
Tel: (410) 956–5771

Michigan Pork Producers Association
4801 Willoughby Road, Suite 5
Holt, MI 48842-1000
Tel: (517) 699–2145
www.mipork.org

Minnesota Pork Board
151 Saint Andrews Court, Suite 810
Mankato, MN 56001
Tel: (507) 345–8814
www.mnpork.com

Mississippi Pork Producers Association
P.O. Box 9815
Mississippi State, MS 39762-9815
Tel: (662) 325–1689

Missouri Pork Producers Association
6235 W. Cunningham Drive
Columbia, MO 65202-9162
Tel: (573) 445–8375
www.mopork.com

Montana Pork Producers Council
County Building MSU Extension
P.O. Box 485
Jordan, MT 59337
Tel: (406) 557–2982

Nebraska Pork Producers Association Inc
P.O. Box 830909
Lincoln, NE 68583-0909
Tel: (402) 472–2563

Nevada Pork Producers Association
38 N. Bybee Lane
Yerington, NV 89447-9708
Tel: (775) 463–5504

New Hampshire Pork Producers Council
206 Currier Road
Hill, NH 03243
Gitchfarm02@yahoo.com

New York Pork Producers Cooperative Inc
4124 MacDougall Road
Waterloo, NY 13165
(315) 585-6276

North Carolina Pork Council Inc
2300 Rexwoods Drive, Suite 340
Raleigh, NC 27607-3361
Tel: (919) 781–0361
www.ncpork.org

North Dakota Pork Council
9905 66th Street SW
Regent, ND 58650
Tel: (701) 563–4513

Ohio Pork Producers Council
5930 Sharon Woods Boulevard, Suite 101
Columbus, OH 43229-2666
Tel: (800) 320–7991
www.ohiopork.org

Oklahoma Pork Council
One North Hudson, Suite 900
Oklahoma City, OK 73102
Tel: (888) 729–7675
www.okpork.org

Oregon Pork Producers Association
7365 Meridian Road NE
Silverton, OR 97381-9188
Tel: (503) 873–5638

Pennsylvania Pork Producers Council
1631 Grim Road
Kutztown, PA 19530-9051
Tel: (610) 285–6519

South Carolina Pork Board
1200 Senate Street, Capitol Complex
Wade-Hampton Building, 5th Floor, Suite 509
Columbia, SC 29211
Tel: (803) 734–2218

South Dakota Pork Producers Council
1404 W. Russell Street
Sioux Falls, SD 57104-1328
Tel: (800) 830–7675
www.sdppc.org

Tennessee Pork Producers Association
13994 Versailles Road
Rockvale, TN 37153
Tel: (615) 274–6533

Texas Pork Producers Association
P.O. Box 10168
Austin, TX 78766
Tel: (800) 501–7675
www.texaspork.org

Utah Pork Producers Association
55 E. 200 North
Providence, UT 84332-9605
Tel: (435) 752–1208
www.utahporkproducers.com

Virginia Pork Industry Association
102 Governor Street, Room 316
Richmond, VA 23219-3642
Tel: (804) 786–7092

Washington Pork Producers
2001 VanTine Road
Garfield, WA 99130-9768
Tel: (509) 397–2694

West Virginia Pork Producers
HC 32 Box 418
Petersburg, WV 26847-9612
wvporkpc@frontiernet.net

Wisconsin Pork Association
9185 Old Potosi Road
Lancaster, WI 53813-0327
Tel: (608) 723–7551
www.wppa.org

Wyoming Pork Producers
P.O. Box 183
Albin, WY 82050
(307) 246–3581

INDEX